M000316234

"*Reading Asha's story will inspire anyone to make changes in their lives and the success they will have with her recipes will convince them that it is possible!* Blissful Mouthful *is everything I look for in a cookbook and even more so in a HEALTHY one. Each recipe is approachable, tasty, nutritious and easily reproduced at home by the individual wishing to make a positive change in their life through the healing powers of food. There are two things that make food great, technique & LOVE and there is plenty of the latter in this book to fill your kitchen, your soul and the bellies of those you cherish! Enjoy!*"
—Jeremy Rock Smith—Executive Chef at Kripalu Center
For Yoga And Health

"*If it were possible to steep heartfelt stories with tantalizing spices, it would be the lovely brew that is* The Blissful Mouthful Cookbook. *With her honest personal accounts and simple wisdom peppered throughout (including tips for saving time and money without compromising health!), Asha Paul has provided what many of us seek: an easy solution to the meal-time-conundrum. Curl up on the couch with a steaming mug of tea, and be ready to flag the recipes you love. Asha Paul is about to take you on a journey of healthy sprinkled with a hearty dose of love.*"
—Laura Thomas—Author, Speaker, Professional Editor

"*This is a delightful collection of simple, nourishing, real food, much of which can be prepared quickly. The ingredients are wholesome, easily found and the flavors are sublime. I am a collector of cookbooks, I've been known to spend hours just flipping through them like magazines on lazy days.* The Blissful Mouth *is a cookbook that is bound to get dog-eared and tomato-stained from constant use, it is a treasure.*"
—Ami Parkerson—Special Sales Manager, New World Library

The Blissful Mouthful Cookbook

Recipes for Your Youthful Life

Simple ❦ Economical ❦ Delicious

ASHA PAUL

INTEGRATIVE NUTRITION HEALTH COACH

DISCLAIMER

The content of this book is for general informational purposes only. It is not meant to be used, nor should it be used, to diagnose or treat any medical condition or to replace the services of your physician or other healthcare provider. The advice and strategies contained in the book may not be suitable for all readers. Please consult your healthcare provider for any questions that you may have about your own medical situation. Neither the author, publisher (Guha Publishing), Guha Soulworks LLC, nor any of their employees or representatives guarantees the accuracy of information in this book or its usefulness to a particular reader, nor are they responsible for any damage or negative consequences that may result from treatment, action taken, or inaction by any person reading or following the information in this book.

To contact the author, visit
ashapaul.com

ISBN: 978-0-578-51723-0

Printed in the United States of America
Photos by: Korey Photography, Austin, TX
Copy Editor: Laura Thomas
Design by: Laura Smyth
Cover Design by: Miladinka Milic
Guha Publishing is a dba of Guha Soulworks LLC

Dedication

To my husband, Russill, the love of my life, my rock and my playmate, and to homecooks everywhere: may you shine bright, and light the path for others to shine as well!

Contents

Introduction

"Let thy food be thy medicine."   HIPPOCRATES

The purpose in writing this book is to empower you, dear reader, with the simple truth that it is your birthright to enjoy abundant health, regardless of your age, gender, and ethnicity. A state of ageless health is always within our grasp, and we quite literally hold it in our hands, as you do this book right now. If your mind is racing with questions of how, what, and when, the answer is: with your ability to create simple and nutritious meals from the comfort of your kitchen.

I invite you to join me in exploring the exciting possibilities of transforming the act of cooking from a chore into a sensual, relaxing, and even a spiritual experience that you can anticipate with pleasure and joy.

My Story

My awakening to the profound relationship between food and health started when a very special person came to live with my husband and I for an extended period after we had moved to America. This person was our mentor, the Rev. Bede Griffiths, a renowned Benedictine monk and Gandalf-like figure (he was in his mid-eighties when he visited us in the year 1990). The first of our extraordinary retreats together took place in the picturesque state of Vermont.

Prior to Fr. Bede's arrival, my husband and I, together with our dear friend, the late Wayne Teasdale, prepared for this special occasion. The rare opportunity of spending three whole months in a private retreat with a world-renowned spiritual teacher was an extraordinary event for the three of us. Preoccupied with our preparations for extended prayer, meditation, and spiritual study, we gave little thought to what we would eat during those three months and how we'd prepare it. Furthermore, no one had the slightest clue about nutrition. And none of us could really cook. We stocked our pantry with soft, delicious bread, white rice (Russill and I practically grew up on it), bags of potatoes, sweetened peanut butter, and jars of jelly. The jelly was a staple for one of our visiting guests who slapped it on everything from toast to omelets to pasta. In addition, we stocked boxes of sugarcoated cereals and a colorful assortment of processed canned foods with little or no nutritional value. Looking back, I am appalled that this is what we anticipated eating for three months.

Discovering the Healing Power of Food

One week after his arrival, Fr. Bede suffered a severe heart arrhythmia. He had had this condition prior to his visit with us and had been placed on heart medication during his travels in Europe. The local physician in Vermont was generous enough to make a house call, but he wanted our mentor to be hospitalized immediately and a pacemaker installed to stabilize his condition. Fr. Bede, with his inimitable English charm, politely but firmly refused the option and asked that we find another solution.

A round of quick phone calls ensued, and we soon found ourselves talking to Dr. Blake Gold who practiced both traditional Chinese medicine as well as nutritional healing. To our complete amazement, we saw our mentor's condition stabilize rapidly, in less than a week, with just herbs and diet and absolutely no medication. Even the previous medication was suspended. The herbs were boiled to make a decoction that was then taken as a tea. The diet was simple, consisting of cooked whole grains, vegetables, and beans. It was this experience that opened my eyes to the extraordinary power of whole foods and their direct relationship to our health and well-being.

My Wake-up Call

Seeing Fr. Bede's health improve dramatically each day inspired us to change our own diet as well. However, this only lasted as long as we were with him. As soon as we dropped him off at the airport, we hit the sugar and white flour like never before, operating on the misconceived logic that our youth would compensate for any nutritional deficiency. We were mistaken. Within a couple of years, I was diagnosed with severe Candidiasis. Fortunately, I consulted an MD who also incorporated sound nutrition to heal me. It was at this point that I made the firm commitment to eating healthy. After my very first doctor's visit, I started to cook simple and healthy meals at home. Needless to say, my health improved spectacularly, and I was inspired to passionately research health and nutrition. Since then, there has been no turning back. This was over twenty-five years ago.

Discernment and Commitment

After years of not knowing how to cook, what to cook, or even wanting to cook, I became obsessed with thoughts of meal preparation. Food and good health became my passion every waking moment, so much so that I started to see it as my life's purpose. This propelled me to study holistic nutrition, which was a real turnaround for me, because ever since the 6th grade my passion was to study engineering.

Between 1986 and 1989, I abandoned my undergraduate studies in Mathematics, fell head over heels in love with a monk, eloped, and came to North America. These changes weren't without difficulty—they caused deep pain to my dear father—but that is another story for another time. From a very early age, I would rather do algebra for hours on end than be caught chopping vegetables. My mother and my in-laws constantly worried about my lack of cooking abilities, and so it took them by surprise when I started taking an avid interest in cooking. Even so, they would not believe for years to come that I could indeed cook, and I became the butt of their jokes.

As I immersed myself in my studies for the next few years, our health (both mine and my husband's) improved significantly. Sore throats, indigestion, headaches, and low energy were things of the past. Even if we did come down with an occasional flu, our recovery time was much quicker than before. More importantly, we felt vibrant, alert, and an overall sense of well-being.

In a nutshell, the fundamental teaching that I gathered from my years of study was this: The body is an intelligent self-healing, self-cleaning, and self-maintaining organism. And with the right kind of nourishment in the form of whole-foods, fresh vegetables, and fruits (preferably organic), our body's healing mechanism is enhanced. Supplements such as vitamins, minerals, and herbs complement our well-being, and are at times necessary; but they are not meant to replace real foods.

The above statement is not meant to imply that western medicine is unimportant. I am a firm believer that allopathic medicine plays a vital role in our welfare. It is arguably the best system in the world when it comes to intervening in traumatic medical events. And with advances in technology and medicine, it can be an amazing blessing. However, an ideal medical system would be one in which conventional medicine openly embraces complementary and alternative healing modalities. It is true that this has happened in integrative and functional medicine—two emerging medical fields in the west—but holistic approaches need to become more mainstream, so that everyone can benefit from a well rounded approach without expensive out of pocket fees, uncertain insurance claims, second guessing, etc. By integrating various healing modalities, we can draw from the best of both worlds without fear and bias.

At the same time, I know and passionately believe that we are each responsible for taking charge of our health and tapping into our innate abilities to heal ourselves, body, mind, and spirit. Then, our doctors become our partners in healing. Without a doubt—from over two decades of personal experience—I know that cooking simple healthy food at home is one of the ways to heal our lives.

Goof-Ups On My Guinea Pig

"A successful marriage isn't the union of two perfect people. It's that of two imperfect people who have learned the value of forgiveness and grace."

DARLENE SCHACHT

My lack of experience was not much help when I began experimenting with healthy cooking. In all my years of growing up in India, I had never stepped into my mother's kitchen, except for the rare occasion to fix a cup of coffee. As I became more conscious, there were no cookbooks that provided tasty, healthy recipes. Additionally, my husband had grown up eating gourmet restaurant food during his entire childhood and teens. My early experiments were quite hard on him. Not only did he have to tolerate the awful taste of my experiments, but he also had to encourage me as I eagerly, but awkwardly, tried to incorporate several cooking techniques all at once in our tiny, dark Californian kitchen. Variations on raw food recipes, foul-tasting green drinks that were invariably drained down the kitchen sink, undercooked macrobiotic meals, quasi Indian foods that were either too spicy or tasteless, or under-baked Italian dishes. These are merely a few of the many disasters too embarrassing to recount. My husband, a truly awesome guy, struggled to maintain his calm and patience with my culinary madness at that time. However, this process of painstaking experimentation led to the refinement of my recipes that I now share with you. And, I am pleased to report to you that, at the present time, my husband not only loves these recipes, making them tried and true, but he gives them a loving stamp of approval in that he now prefers eating at home to eating in restaurants!

Kudos From a Gastronome

As my cooking improved, my husband's taste buds were more than satisfied. I saw this as a momentous feat, since, as mentioned, Russill was practically raised on gourmet restaurant meals! Despite growing up in a strong meat-eating family who devoured any form of animal flesh, land or sea, Russill astonishingly remained a vegetarian since the age of four, when he adamantly refused to partake in any form of meat-based food. His indulgent parents, although distressed by their son's quirkiness, gave in. As long as he ate his quarter boiled egg every morning, he had free rein to remain a vegetarian, and his meals came (lunch, supper, and sometimes breakfast) from kosher vegetarian restaurants. Thus, he developed a fine taste for gourmet food from a very tender age.

The tension between adhering to my nutritional knowledge, together with the need to satisfy my husband's palate, has resulted in the wonderful recipes that I now share with you. Also, as a busy professional, I need my cooking time to be efficient, not laborious.

Food and Hormones

As my body ages, balancing my hormones is crucial for my well-being. Almost every woman in her late thirties, forties, fifties, and beyond knows how unnerving and scary this phase can be. The hormonal roller coaster can take over our lives and wreak havoc on our bodies. Not only are we dealing with the hormonal changes that affect us biologically and psychologically, but we are literally undergoing physical changes as well—least of all the crow's feet and that ever-deepening smile line. I have been deeply humbled, awed, and at times terrified to see the power of food directly related to my moods, energy, and even that deepening smile line! By trial and error I have learned to work with and embrace certain foods that nurture and soothe my hormones. And sadly, certain favorite foods had to be eliminated altogether. Has it been worth it? The answer is a resounding YES! It has made me a believer without a shred of doubt that what we put in our mouth has a direct correlation to our over all well-being: physical, emotional, psychological, and spiritual.

Homemade Versus Restaurant Meals

With our current lifestyle habits and easily accessible fast food restaurants, preparing meals at home has and continues to drop to the bottom of our priority list. If we are serious about maintaining a healthy body and mind, nutritious home-cooked meals cannot be replaced by high-end restaurants or frozen dinners from the supermarket. Additionally, home-cooked meals cost less, which is a nice bonus even when money is not a concern. The extra savings can be used for a nice massage or a spa day, or tithed to your favorite charity.

Of course, there's a reason we turn to restaurants or fast food joints at the end of a long, hard day. It feels easier to reach for packaged frozen or prepackaged foods, restaurant takeout, or something hastily thrown together that is neither tasty nor nutritious. But hang on—I have a few simple, but effective, ways you can tackle this issue. One option is to get your family involved. It is a great way to bond at the end of the day. You can engage in lively conversation, and before you know it, you've created a meal together. If you live by yourself or are unable to get your family involved, this is your chance to start looking at cooking from a whole new perspective of self-care and self-love. How? See below...

A Conscious Act of Transformation

> *"The greatest discovery of all time is that a person can change his future by merely changing his attitude."*
> OPRAH WINFREY

Cooking can feel like a chore, especially if we are dealing with a full-time career, children, family, or other commitments that claim our time and attention. As discussed in the previous section, we would rather rely on restaurant meals and fast food to eliminate time spent in the kitchen. I was no exception, until it dawned on me that I was letting go of a precious opportunity to care for my family and myself. I realized I could improve my health and the health of those I love with just a bit of planning and a slight change in attitude. This made a world of a difference in the way I approached cooking. I no longer regarded it as a chore, but as a form of creative expression. All I needed was an attitude adjustment! Seriously, this really worked like a charm. And you cannot always rely on your family to help. When they do, it is awesome. But cooking can also be a joyous form of self-care.

Thus, cooking becomes a delightfully transformative act, especially when we approach the process with clear intentions.

I love my work with all my heart (my husband and I have been serving people using spiritual methodologies to transform their lives for the past twenty years). But I confess, preparing and cooking our meals at home on a regular basis makes me feel that I have achieved something significant for the day despite my busy work schedule, and it bestows a deep sense of fulfillment. It is truly gratifying to know that I am being proactive about our health on a daily basis.

Personally, cooking has served as a great source of creative expression for me. Unlike my husband, I do not create beautiful music; but when I cook, I feel like I am an artist in my own right. To be able to put together a meal from scratch and to see my loved ones enjoy it is a source of pure joy. Also, we are no longer subject to the guessing game. What do I mean by this? When you cook, you have first hand knowledge of what exactly went into creating your meal—what kind of oil, what kind of additives (if any at all), how much salt, the cooking method, deep fried, sautéed, etc.

Just to clarify, I do believe both genders (men and women) must cook healthy meals and share the cooking responsibility at home, especially if both are working full-time. It should not be just the women's responsibility. But two facts that I would like to bring to your attention are:

a) The majority of women call the household's financial shots[1]
b) Only 10% of Americans cook at home[2]

So ladies, let's change the second fact and make it a priority to incorporate home cooking as part of our healthy lifestyle.

Strategies to Save Time and Money

My cooking style is simple with an emphasis on minimizing food preparation, without compromising health or taste. In addition, I try to leverage the time spent cooking by making double or triple the quantity so that I have ready-to-go home-cooked meals. This saves both time and money in the long run. Especially during weekends, I often double the quantity for certain dishes such as grains and beans (as a matter of fact, beans taste better the next day because the flavors have had time to blend in). The extra time spent preparing the larger quantities (chopping and blending) is hardly noticeable, but the returns are well worth it, as we have great meals that only need heating, and voila! Ready to eat! This does not mean that we do not treat ourselves to restaurant meals, but it does mean we can prioritize eating healthy even on busy weeks days, without much fuss.

My one golden rule is to avoid cooking greens or making salads with greens in advance. They are best prepared fresh and can be made in less than ten minutes.

I truly believe planning our meals ahead of time is a fundamental component to maintaining our ideal body weight without going on fad diets and feeling deprived. More than just keeping our ideal weight, we nourish our bodies and minds with nature's wholesome goodness and better-for-you naturally delicious food.

Sacred Kitchen = Sacred Home

Figuratively and literally speaking, the kitchen is the most nourishing place in a home. Not only is it the place where we cook our meals, but it's also the space where our relationships nurture us. Some of our most healing conversations with a spouse or a lover, son or daughter, mother or father happen around our kitchen tables. And some of our best moments laughing with friends and family happen in kitchens, where there's an air of informality.

Food, cooking, healing, and relationships go together. Michael Pollan (one of my favorite authors) wrote in his powerful book *Cooked*, which is also a four-part documentary, "In ancient Greece, the word for 'cook,' 'butcher,' and 'priest' was the same — mageiros — and the word shares an etymological root with 'magic.'"

In India, the kitchen in a Hindu household (around 248 million homes) is considered sacred. As a matter of fact, many millions of Indians in India live in homes that are two rooms or less. And almost every Hindu kitchen, no matter how small or poor, will have a space allocated for a shrine. The shrine will consist of an image or images of a goddess, a small oil lamp, fresh flowers (whenever possible), and incense. In a traditional Hindu household, the oil lamp is lit every morning— usually before the crack of dawn—by the woman of the house after her early morning shower, commonly referred to as a bath. As a side note, the term "bath" is not to be confused with soaking in a bathtub, like how we do it in the west, but more of a bucket bath, which basically consists of filling a steel or plastic bucket with water and using a small mug to pour the water over your body.

Believe me, it is hygienic, relaxing, and conserves water! I prefer and indulge in bucket baths every year, when we journey to India with a group of westerners for our annual pilgrimage, even though the places where we stay have working showers.

Now back to our Hindu kitchen ritual: the lighting of the lamp and the burning of incense symbolize invoking the goddess's blessing and honoring her before any food or drink is prepared for the day. Also, it is common to have Sanskrit chanting in the background, which creates an auspicious atmosphere. It is understood that the sacred chanting not only creates a sacred space with its holy vibrations, but also infuses the food with healing qualities. I do something similar every morning in our home in the US (even though I did not grow up in a Hindu household; my birth family is Christian). It makes a tremendous difference not only in the quality of the space in which we cook, but also in the energy of our home and the food we eat. With these simple rituals, the kitchen is now transformed into a sacred space, and the relationship between the material and the spiritual is soundly established for the day.

The Goddess: Patron of the Culinary Art

According to Hindu mythology, there's a story that takes place at the dawn of civilization. One fine summer afternoon, Lord Shiva, one of the gods of the Hindu pantheon (also considered the supreme deity by many millions of Hindus), finds himself reclining in his heavenly Himalayan abode beside his beautiful wife, goddess Parvati. As they lounge around, reveling in each other's company, Shiva, out of the blue, turns to Parvati and declares that the notion of food is an illusion and that human beings can very well subsist without it.

Now, Parvati, an aspect of the absolute divine feminine, is the power and the expression behind the material world (food being an integral part of this domain). She was a smart woman who could indulge her husband's ego from time to time, letting things slide, but not this instance. She was seething inside. Her thoughts were something in this vein: "The audacity of the man! And, too, after a sumptuous meal I lovingly and painstakingly prepared. This is indeed a teaching moment!" Without saying a word, Parvati gently disengaged from Shiva's embrace, stepped off their marital bed, draped her slender shoulder with a luxurious Pashmina shawl, and, with a cool dignity, walked out of the room, Shiva's life, and planet earth!

In no time, her disappearance was felt acutely, not only by Shiva, but the whole world. The earth, a manifestation of the divine feminine, became desolate and arid. People starved, desperate for food. Shiva, with all his might and power, was unable to reverse the situation. Finally, the compassionate Parvati, moved by her people's plight, (it certainly wasn't their fault), opened up a kitchen in the holy city of Kashi (known today as Varnasi) and began her feeding mission. The news reached Shiva, who made haste to Kashi, where he duly repented and humbly acknowledged his wife's power. Parvati forgave Shiva wholeheartedly, fed him with her own hands, and all was well between them, and hence on planet earth. From that day onwards, Shiva decreed that Parvati be worshipped as Annapurna, the goddess of nourishment and everything related to food. To date,

Annapurna is a revered goddess and temples are dedicated to her worship.

This is a fabulous story, for the obvious reason that it places women on an equal footing with men, and also because it establishes the fundamental relationship between humans, the divine, and the natural world. Throughout history, cultures around the world have understood and honored this fundamental relationship and celebrated it through the medium of food. It is time to revive this simple but profound awareness and establish our own meaningful connections to whole foods, healing, and health. Especially as we push our carts down supermarket aisles filled with so called "food," most of which is unfit for human consumption.

Fundamentals For Healthy Cooking and Eating

"As I see it, every day you do one of two things: build health or produce disease in yourself."[3]

ADELLE DAVIS

Ms. Davis is considered a pioneer in nutritional health, and thus endearingly nicknamed "the first lady of nutrition."

Our increasing obesity epidemic across the world has created a frantic reaction. Some of us are obsessed with finding the right diet to combat the issue of ever increasing waistlines. But what is a perfect diet?

Let's look at what the experts have to say, starting with Dr. Walter Willett. Dr. Willet has been the chair of the department of nutrition at the Harvard School of Public Health for 25 long years (1991 to 2017) and is currently the Fredrick John Stare Professor of Epidemiology and Nutrition at the Harvard School of Public Health. He says, "The real issue is not losing weight—people can cut back on calories and lose weight on almost any diet—but keeping weight off over the long run. Thus, it is more important to find a way of eating that you can stay with for the rest of your life."[4]

Dr. Mehmet Oz is a heart surgeon who specializes in heart transplants and minimally invasive procedures, and is world-renowned for his famous TV show, "The Dr. Oz Show." He was one of the guest teachers during my health coaching training program, and passionately taught us about how belly fat is a major health concern. Waist— not weight—drives health issues. He also spoke about how he told most of his patients to go on a diet, but it didn't work. He said, "In clinical trial, every weight loss approach, every diet works, and they all fail, because they are all difficult to do. Therefore, the question is what will work for you forever." In other words, diets do not work for the long term because what sustains is lifestyle, not diet.

Those are powerful words. It is crucial that you understand, and so I will say it again: **DIETS DO NOT WORK!** They are dime a dozen, and I have studied over a 100 different dietary theories ranging from the book *Japanese Women Don't Get Old or Fat*, to vegan, paleo, low-calorie, low-cholesterol, low-protein, low-carbohydrate, and more. Although each of these dietary theories is based on sound scientific principles and a lot of solid nutritional advise, they have pros and cons. Ninety-five percent of dieters gain back the weight they lost, plus more.

Dieting is deeply imbedded in our society. We are brainwashed from a very young age to think dieting is the way to solve issues with our bodies. This message has ruinous effects, especially on young girls and women. This is not to say that men are not affected, as they too have eating disorders, although we don't recognize them as often.

As appalling as it may sound, our kids, even toddlers, are targeted by the fast food industry. The idea is to start them young with the lure of toys and an environment that mimics a child's paradise in order to make them customers for life using powerful emotional hooks.[5] None of us want this for our children! Consciously and unconsciously, our lifestyle choices and eating habits are determined by media and advertising. Major corporations have hijacked our food industry and agricultural practices. Dietary basics, such as fruits and vegetables, are being classified as specialty foods. More than ever before, we need to be aware of which influences we allow to shape our behaviors. We can't rely on big industries to make healthy choice for us.

Instead, we need to focus on different lifestyle habits by making gradual, steady change until healthy living is second nature. This way, we give up dieting for good and focus on what food and beverages are good for our bodies and mind so that we can thrive and age well.

I am passionate about aging well and helping others to do the same. I turned 50 in 2018. And I love working with my senior clients, part of which involves helping them maintain their ideal weight and a trimmer waistline.

Please keep in mind that one of the secrets to eating healthy depends on the concept of Bio-individuality,[6] which simply means finding the unique way of eating that suits your specific body.

A wise quote to remember when it comes to

changing habits is Mark Twain's: *"Habit is habit and not to be flung out of the window by anyone, but coaxed downstairs a step at a time."*

The recipes in this book are mainly created to cook nutritious meals in your kitchen regularly and enjoy it without sacrificing taste.

Tips To Make Cooking Purposeful & Enjoyable

Get your family involved. This not only reduces the food preparation (peeling, chopping, blending, etc.) time, but more importantly helps bring family members closer together emotionally, thus strengthening the family bond. It also helps with picky eaters, especially children! When children are not involved with their food,they can grow up to be picky eaters as a result. Research shows that this can change when children become involved with food preparation. The same can happen with adults.

Cooking together can be therapeutic. In her book *The Path of Practice*, Maya Tiwari shares a powerful story of a nine-year-old girl with an eating disorder. What turned it around for the little girl, after multiple forms of failed treatments, was the simple, therapeutic act of grinding spices together with her mother before meals.

If you're cooking solo, some exciting cooking activities include listening to your favorite music, audio books, podcast, etc.

I would be remiss if I do not mention chanting mantras or listening to positive affirmations as powerful cooking rituals. Our thoughts and emotions go into the food we prepare, so infusing the food with positive vibrations is a great practice.

Omnivore vs. Vegetarian

"You are what you eat eats."   MICHAEL POLLAN

With over a hundred diets that bombard us—often times with conflicting messages and advise—one of the most fiercely debated issues is the consumption of animal protein. It is healthy or not? Is veganism healthier than eating paleo? Both sides provide influential reasons and arguments as to why their way of eating is superior and healthier.

Many medical doctors, including Dr. Dean Ornish, one of the leading cardiovascular health experts in the United States, Dr. Joel Fuhrman, known for his nutritarian diet, and Dr. Neal Barnard, who is a cardiologist and the president of the Physicians Committee for Responsible Medicine, recommend a plant-based diet. Eating mostly plants can help prevent and reverse many degenerative diseases such as diabetes, heart disease, arthritis, and certain forms of cancer.

On the ethical and ecological front, we have great thinkers like Michael Pollan, who writes extensively about food and culture. He has written at least four *New York Times* bestsellers, and his popular book *In Defense of Food* starts with these insightful words: "Eat food. Not too much. Mostly Plants."

There are equally well-known and high profiles doctors such Dr. Mark Hyman (as of this writing, he is the chairman of functional medicine) and Dr. William Davis, a cardiologist who wrote the *New York Times* bestseller *Wheat Belly*, who suggest a diet that includes humanely, pasture-raised animal protein.

So, my dear reader, what are you to do? What is the best diet for you and your family? Are you confused or frustrated? Welcome to the club, my friend.

It is my heartfelt desire and hope, that my story below will serve as a guidepost to you.

As mentioned earlier, I grew up in India. My family was—and still are—a minority community: Roman Catholics. We ate meat in a predominately vegetarian country. So I grew up eating meat; chicken and shrimp were my favorites. At the age of eighteen I met my mentor Fr. Bede Griffiths, a catholic monk and priest who was the leader of a unique ashram where the monks were Christian in their faith, but adopted Hindu culture, including vegetarianism. So from the age of eighteen into my mid-forties, I remained a strict vegetarian (with very few lapses). As a matter of fact, my husband and I ate more vegan than vegetarian.

At the age of 39, I was diagnosed with serve uterine fibroids (extremely painful periods, heavy bleeding every 26 days, and extremely low iron for years) and hypothyroidism. I still refused to give up my way of eating, despite my nutritional knowledge and numerous medical and alternative health care practitioners ardently advising me to include a small quantity of high quality animal protein into my diet. So what gave? At the age of 45, a false Pap smear scare followed by a biopsy and the very likely possibility of losing my uterus made me to include humanely-raised animal protein into my diet.

A Part-Time Vegetarian

When we first arrived in the US, my husband Russill and I stayed in a semi-monastic community where our dear friend Wayne Teasdale was a longtime resident. Witnessing our vegetarianism, Wayne wanted to give it a try, but he was not going to do it silently. He announced to everyone in the community that he, too, was going to be a vegetarian, giving up all meat, including chicken (his all time favorite). One evening during our communal supper, Russill needed to use the restroom. Noticing the restroom door slightly ajar, Russill pushed it open and found Wayne hastily gobbling down a large leg of chicken, gravy dripping down his chin. Russill cracked up. "Vegetarian, huh?" Russill teased. And Wayne, with his typical Irish wit and inimitable charm, sheepishly said, "I forgot to mention that I was only going to be a part-time vegetarian."

The moral of the story is if you are trying to switch from a predominantly meat-based diet to a vegetarian one but find it difficult, try being a part-time vegetarian. It can work!

Compared to other scientific fields, nutritional science is young,[7] reductionist in its approach, and messy[8] because of conflicts of interest, meaning food companies and related industrial groups sponsor research. The result is we, the unsuspecting consumers, are constantly bombarded with confusing new information and polarized opinions not necessarily based on facts. But one thing that almost all experts and health practitioners who embrace nutritional therapy agree on is this: a predominantly plant-based diet is a healthier lifestyle choice.

With this in mind I have outlined a simple plan you can implement if you desire to increase your intake of veggies:

For the first week, focus on adding whole fruits and veggies (fresh or frozen) to your meals in addition to your meat and poultry dishes. Try to do this even during breakfast time. For example, if you are used to eating eggs for breakfast, make it a veggie omelet by adding baby spinach, bell pepper, green onions, fresh herbs, etc. to your eggs.

For the second week, make two to three meals per week vegan or vegetarian. If you plan on eating dairy, go easy on the cheese, as the common tendency is to substitute meat with dairy products.

For the third week, try alternating between being a vegan or vegetarian for an entire day, and the following day have two vegan or vegetarian meals and a small-sized portion of meat (or poultry or fish) along with fresh veggies for your third meal.

The idea is to increase your consumption of a variety of vegetables, fruits that could be fresh or frozen, and whole foods while minimizing consuming excessive amounts of animal protein and processed foods.

Please note: the above guidelines are not prescriptive. Be sure to consult your physician (or health-care practitioner) before changing your diet.

If it is within your budget, opt for organic, humanely raised poultry, eggs, and meat, free of additives and minimal processing If it is not within your budget to buy organic, then be sure to visit the Environmental Working Group's website—www.ewg.org—and click on the following links to learn more:

1. "Shopper's Guide to Pesticides in Produce"
2. "Meat Eaters Guide to Climate Change and Health"

Another good resource is greenerchoices.org, a non-profit organization that works with consumers to create a safer and healthier world.

Tenets of The Blissful Mouthful Way

The reason I chose "Blissful Mouthful" is to impress upon the reader that healthy cooking and eating is pleasurable, and needs to remain so to become a lifestyle. This has been my lifestyle for the past 25 years, and I hope it will become yours and your loved ones. Finally, before we delve into the recipes, let me share with you the Tenets of the Blissful Mouthful Way:

1. Good health is our birthright, regardless of age.
2. Health and fitness begin in the kitchen.
3. Consider the pros and cons of your food before eating it.
4. Our fingers, forks, and knives are like sacred vessels we bring to the altar of good health, to feed the life within us.
5. Eat a plant-based diet consisting of whole foods. When consuming animal protein, ensure ethical and humane practices are in place.
6. Cooking is an act of therapeutic transformation that nourishes and strengthens family bonds.
7. True, lasting change is established by how we think, and our willingness to co-create our health and happiness with our inner wisdom.

Cooking Tips & Techniques

Cooking Tips & Techniques

The recipes in this book are predominately vegan-friendly, with a few exceptions.

My goal in writing this book is to encourage you to incorporate a wide range of whole foods, ideally farm-to-table, regularly. Further, I wish to invite you to view our kitchens as a sacred playground where simple, homecooked meals can help us transform and heal our bodies, minds, and souls.

Unlease your creativity, have fun experimenting with my recipes, and offer your feedback via my Facebook page. Details on connecting with me are provided toward the end of this book under the title "Author's Bio."

Popping Mustard Seeds:

Place a skillet or sauté pan on high heat and add mustard seeds. As the seeds begin to pop, remove the pan from heat and swirl the pan so the seeds pop evenly.

If you are new to popping mustard seeds, I suggest that you get a splatter guard and cover the skillet or the sauté pan before the seeds begin to pop. Once you get used to it, you can do without the splatter guard. Depending on your stovetop, it usually take about a 2 to 3 minutes after placing the pan on high heat before the seeds begin popping.

Dry Roasting Seeds and Spices:

Place a small cast iron skillet or a stainless steel sauté pan on medium heat and warm the pan for 30 to 45 seconds. Add the required quantity of seeds and, with the help of a wooden spoon, move the seeds around for about 30 to 45 seconds. Once the seeds begin to change color and start producing an aromatic smell, turn off heat, move the skillet to a cooler surface, and let it cool before grinding it into a powder.

Water Technique:

For some of the recipes, especially while sautéing on high heat, I suggest sprinkling small amounts of water to avoid burning the veggies. The trick is to eyeball the quantity of water and stir the veggies around the sauté pan in quick and fast movements. I keep a small bowl of water near me and use my fingers to sprinkle the water.

Cooking Time:

Cooking time, especially when related to boiling soups, etc., excludes the time required to bring the soup to a boil, as this would depend on your stovetop as well the kind of fuel you're using (i.e. electricity or gas).

Utensils:

Ideally, you want to use non-reactive utensils, such as stainless steel or glass ware. Likewise, if you opt to use canned products, such as tomatoes, try purchasing products that are packaged in bottles or look for BPA-free cans.

Soaking Grains and Beans:

Yes, soaking your grains, lentils, and beans is recommended. In the beginning this concept might appear labor-intensive and unnecessary. The reason why we soak these nutritional gems is to increase digestibility and to reduce phytic acid.

By the way, phytic acid tends to bind to essential minerals (iron, zinc, calcium, magnesium) and hinders the body's ability to absorb them.

Oils:

The recipes in this book recommend using extra virgin olive oil, virgin coconut oil, avocado oil. Some salad recipes include toasted sesame oil for flavor. However, if you prefer to avoid using toasted seasame oil, do so. For the past several years, coconut oil has been the darling of the health market. But in the year 2017, the American Heart Association came out with an advisory report cautioning against coconut oil. Of course, coconut oil proponents say otherwise.

I personally like using a moderate amount of coconut oil, especially to sauté and sometimes to fry things. I will let you be the judge and choose wisely.

Organic vs Non-Organic:

I recommend organic ingredients as much as possible. However, I understand that there are two main reasons why people hesitate: cost and availability.

Just so you know, when I decided to eat all organic in the mid 90's, our standard of living was below the poverty line. Because eating organic was a top priority for me, I learned to prioritize our expenses, and I haven't looked back since.

Even if you don't eat all organic, be sure to become familiar with the dirty dozen list by periodically visiting The Environmental Working Group's website (www.ewg.org).

Use of Pressure Cooker:

This baby is a true treasure and a time-saver. Once you fall in love with the pressure cooker, it becomes indispensable. Vegetables like squash, beets, and turnips can also be cooked in the pressure cooker for a short time, especially when making soups. If you plan on using one, follow the safety information and time chart.

Now, let's get cooking, my friend!

Salads

Carrot Beet Salad

The quantity below can easily serve six people. If you are a household of three or less, you can store the balance in the fridge. It actually tastes better the next day, as the marinated flavors have had time to settle in.

This salad could serve as a base, meaning you could make a large batch and add fresh spinach, microgreens or baby greens (kale, arugula, lettuce, etc.) when you want to fix yourself a salad.

Consuming beets on a regular basis is very beneficial; they are considered a superfood for the brain and help lower blood pressure, among other health benefits.

Ingredients:
5 medium carrots, scrubbed and grated
2 small beets, peeled and grated

Ingredients for the dressing:
½ teaspoon ginger, peeled and finely grated
1 tablespoon extra virgin olive oil
1 tablespoon raw apple cider vinegar
    (preferably organic)
1 Thai chili pepper, seeded and minced
    (optional)
Juice of 1 lemon
2 to 3 drops stevia

Freshly ground black pepper
Sea salt to taste
1 tablespoon raw black sesame seeds

1. Place all of the dressing ingredients (except for the sesame seeds) in large salad bowl and blend well with a fork or a whisk.
2. Add the grated veggies and incorporate well into the dressing.
3. Cover and let the salad sit at room temperature for 30 to 45 minutes.
4. Sprinkle the sesame seeds, mix well and serve

Note: If you are opting not to include the Thai chili pepper, you may also want to avoid using stevia as well.

Green Apple-Zucchini Salad

PREPARATION TIME: 15 MINUTES

It you are not a fan of raw cilantro leaves (like Julia Child), you can substitute Thai basil or mint leaves. Thai basil (has purple stems) will impart a stronger flavor on the salad. I have experimented with all three options (cilantro, Thai basil, and mint leaves) and my preference is cilantro leaves.

Ingredients:
1 medium carrot, scrubbed and diced
1 small zucchini, diced
3 Easter radish, grated
3 sun dried tomatoes soaked in olive oil, diced
2 cups baby spinach, rinsed and dried
1 medium green apple, diced

Ingredients for the dressing:
½ inch ginger peeled and made into a paste
    (use mortar and pestle or a small blender,
    like Rocket or Bullet, to make the paste)
¼ teaspoon red chili flakes (optional)
1 tablespoon organic virgin coconut oil
Juice of 1 lime
Sea salt to taste
1 tablespoon cilantro leaves, minced
2 tablespoons raw sunflower seeds

1. Place all of the dressing ingredients (except for the sunflower seeds) in large salad bowl and blend well, with the help of a fork or whisk.
2. Add the diced and grated veggies, spinach, and the diced green apple into the dressing and toss well.
3. Cover and let sit in room temperature for 45 minutes to an hour.
4. Sprinkle the sunflower seeds, give it a good mix and serve.

Note: Making the ginger into a paste instead of grating helps the flavors integrate.

Jicama Coleslaw

If you are not familiar with jicama, you are in for a treat. It is also known as Mexican yam or Mexican turnip. It is a root vegetable packed with healthy nutrients and has a sweet flavor and a crunchy texture.

I use tahini (sesame seed paste) instead of mayonnaise in my version of coleslaw, and it is on the spicy side. You may reduce or skip the Thai pepper for a milder taste. You may also substitute tahini with almond butter for a different flavor.

Ingredients:
1 cup green cabbage, finely shredded
1 small carrot, scrubbed and finely diced
1 small jicama, peeled and finely diced
7 jumbo black olives, finely diced

Ingredients for the dressing:
2 tablespoons tahini paste (preferably organic)
1 inch ginger, peeled and cut into pieces
3 tablespoons filtered water
1 small Thai pepper, seeded
1 tablespoon extra virgin organic olive oil
2 tablespoons fresh lemon juice
¼ teaspoon red chili powder
3 drops stevia (optional)
Sea salt to taste

1. Blend the tahini paste, lemon juice, water, olive oil, ginger, Thai pepper (if using), red chili powder, and sea salt in a blender for about 60 to 90 seconds. Add more water if the paste is too thick.
2. Pour the blended tahini paste into veggies and fold in the dressing to coat the veggies. Cover the bowl airtight and refrigerate for at least 2 to 3 hours before serving.

Note: The longer the cabbage marinates in the dressing the tastier it gets. Once you mix in the cabbage with the dressing, taste to see if you need to add more lemon juice.

Spinach Salad

PREPARATION TIME: 15 MINUTES

This is one of our go-to salads, especially during busy work weekday nights. The dressing can be made in advance and used for the next few days—just increase the quantity.

If you are using garlic in the dressing and want to make it ahead of time, store the dressing in the refrigerator.

Ingredients:
2 cups baby spinach leaves, rinsed and dried
1 small tomato, thinly sliced
½ red bell pepper, thinly sliced
¼ purple onion, thinly sliced
4 pimento stuffed green olives, thinly sliced

Ingredients for the dressing:
1 tablespoon raw apple cider vinegar
1 tablespoon extra virgin organic olive oil
½ teaspoon toasted sesame oil
1 small clove garlic, peeled and crushed or
    grated (optional)
Freshly cracked black pepper to taste
Sea salt to taste
2 tablespoons sliced almonds (raw)

1. Rinse the spinach and drain; pat dry if necessary.
2. Place the dressing ingredients in a large bowl and blend well, with the help of a fork or whisk.
3. Add the prepared veggies to the salad dressing and coat the veggies with dressing.
4. Garnish the salad with sliced almonds and serve.

Black Bean Salad

This superfood salad can be eaten as is, or you can use it as stuffing for pita pockets or tortilla wraps. It is quick to make and simply delicious. It is kind of unusual to blend in beans as part of a salad dressing, but think of it as black bean hummus, if you will!

I'm partial to romaine lettuce, but feel free to substitute lettuce of your choice.

Ingredients:
16 ounces baby spinach, washed and
    drained well
3 large romaine lettuce leaves, chopped or
    torn apart
1 small carrot, scrubbed and finely grated
1 small beet, finely grated
2 ribs celery, chopped

Ingredients for blending:
12 ounces cooked black beans
4 sun-dried tomatoes (soaked in oil is fine)
4 ounces pitted black olives
2 tablespoons almond butter (or nut butter
    of your choice)
2 tablespoons lemon juice
1 teaspoon red chili flakes
2 cloves garlic, peeled
1 tablespoon organic extra virgin olive oil

Freshly cracked black pepper to taste
Sea salt to taste
½ cup filtered water

For garnishing:
½ teaspoon toasted sesame oil
2 tablespoons raw pumpkin seeds

1. Soak the sun-dried tomatoes (if using un-soaked ones) in ½ cup of water for 30 minutes or so. Use the soaked water when blending.
2. Using a blender or food processor, blend all the ingredients listed for blending into a smooth paste. Add extra water if necessary to dilute the paste. The desired consistency should neither be runny nor too thick.
3. Place the prepared vegetables in a large mixing bowl; add the blended paste, toss well.
4. Sprinkle the pumpkins seeds over the salad and drizzle with toasted sesame oil. Serve.

Note: If you are cooking your beans at home and not using canned beans, follow this method for an added zing.

Soak beans over night. Rinse several times. Place the beans in the cooking pot or a pressure cooker, add sea salt to taste, 2 whole cloves, 2 teaspoon cumin seeds, and cook for 12 minutes.

Once the beans are cool enough to handle, rinse the beans well with room temperature filtered water. If you can pick out the cloves from the beans, great; if not, don't bother. Drain the beans well before blending it with the other ingredients.

Roasted Onion Salad

Pan roasted onions and bell peppers are a great addition to salad greens, especially when you don't feel like eating your greens. Additionally, corn kernels and walnuts make this dish feel like a one-pot meal. Enjoy!

Ingredients:
½ cup red onion, roughly chopped
½ cup red bell pepper (or yellow or orange), roughly chopped
2 tablespoons fresh or frozen corn kernels (preferably organic)
1 large head of butter lettuce (or lettuce of your choice), torn apart into bite size pieces

Ingredients for the dressing:
1 tablespoon balsamic vinegar
¾ tablespoon organic virgin coconut oil
¾ tablespoon organic extra virgin olive oil
Freshly ground black pepper
Sea salt to taste
2 tablespoons raw walnuts chopped

1. Place a large cast iron skillet on high heat and warm it for 60 to 90 seconds.
2. Add the chopped onions, and then the coconut oil and roast on high heat for one minute.
3. Add the bell peppers and continue roasting for an additional three minutes. Reduce heat to medium-high, if necessary.
4. Add the frozen or fresh corn kernels and roast for 30 to 45 seconds. Turn off heat and place the roasted veggies in a large salad bowl; season with salt and let it cool.
5. Place a small cast iron skillet on medium-high heat. Slowly add the balsamic vinegar and the olive oil and let it warm for about a minute. Turn off heat.
6. Add the chopped or torn lettuce to the roasted and cooled veggies, and pour the warmed balsamic and olive oil mixture over the veggies.
7. Season it with freshly crushed black pepper, sprinkle the chopped walnuts, toss well and serve.

Warm Chickpea Salad

This is one of our favorite ways to eat chickpeas. The sautéed onions and the garam masala enhance the flavor of the chickpeas, making it exotic yet super simple to prepare.

It's amazingly filling, and you can eat it as a main dish, or serve it as a side.

I am not a big fan of garam masala, as I find the flavors too intense, but I like to keep a small amount in my spice drawer, especially for this salad.

By the way, if you are not familiar with garam masala, it is a blended Indian spice mixture that mainly consists of cumin, coriander, black or white pepper, cinnamon, bay leaf, and cloves. It can be purchased from Whole Foods or from any Indian grocery stores.

Ingredients:
1 cup cooked chickpeas
½ cup red onions, chopped
¾ teaspoon garlic powder
¾ teaspoon garam masala powder
2 tablespoons tomato puree (preferably organic)
1½ tablespoons organic virgin coconut oil (or
    avocado oil)
Sea salt to taste
2 medium sized head of romaine lettuce or
    lettuce of your choice

1. Place a large iron skillet on medium heat for 60 to 90 seconds.
2. Add the chopped onions and 1 tablespoon of coconut oil (or avocado oil). Increase to high heat and sauté for three minutes, stirring constantly, so the onions don't burn.
3. Add the spices, pureed tomato paste, and the chickpeas, and continue sautéing for another two minutes. Add a teaspoon or more of water if necessary to avoid burning the onions.
4. Turn off heat and add the chopped lettuce and the remaining oil (½ teaspoon). Season with sea salt and mix well. Serve immediately.

Cucumber Salad

PREPARATION TIME: 10 MINUTES

This super simple salad can be made in no time and can be eaten as a snack all by itself. I prefer to use English cucumbers, as they are almost seedless, meaning their seeds are hardly noticeable, unlike regular cucumbers, which often have hard, large seeds that can be bitter.

Ingredients:
1 large English cucumber peeled and cut into thin ½ moon slices

Ingredients for the dressing:
½ inch ginger, peeled and grated
1 teaspoon cumin powder
2 tablespoons lemon juice
1 teaspoon toasted sesame oil
¼ teaspoon red chili flakes (optional)
1 teaspoon mint leaves, minced

1. Place all of the dressing ingredients, with the exception of the mint leaves, in large salad bowl and blend well, with the help of a fork or whisk.
2. Add the sliced cucumber and the mint leaves to the dressing and toss well.
3. Cover the bowl airtight and refrigerate for at least 30 minutes before serving.

Soups

Cumin Scented Beet Soup

PREPARATION TIME: 15 MINUTES
COOKING TIME: 5 MINUTES

This hearty soup is quick and simple to prepare. It is great on a cold, wintery day. The coconut milk enriches the flavor of the beets, the spices balance the sweetness of the beets, and the brown rice gives body to the soup.

Grating the beets reduces the cooking time. If you are not a beet lover (I have some coaching clients who really don't like them), this soup might convert you!

Ingredients:
1 medium beet, peeled and grated
2 garlic cloves, peeled and minced
1 green chili, seeded and minced
1 teaspoon cumin seeds, crushed
1 teaspoon black mustard seeds
¼ teaspoon turmeric powder
1 teaspoon organic virgin coconut oil
¼ cup coconut milk
Freshly ground black pepper to taste (optional)
Sea salt to taste
1 tablespoon lime juice1 tablespoon cooked
    brown rice
1 cup filtered water
1 tablespoon fresh basil leaves, minced

1. Place a heavy bottomed stainless steel soup pot on high heat. After 60 seconds or so, add the mustard seeds and pop them. Add the oil, chili, garlic, cumin seeds, and the turmeric powder. Sauté on high heat for about a minute. Be very mindful not to burn the spices, reduce heat if necessary.
2. Add the grated beets and continue sautéing for another minute. Now pour in the coconut milk, water, sea salt, and freshly cracked black pepper (if using), bring to a quick boil, add the brown rice and the cilantro leaves, turn off heat, add the lime juice, cover and let the soup sit on the stovetop for 3 to 5 minutes before serving.

Notes: Use a mortar and pestle or spice grinder to crush the cumin seeds. If using the spice grinder, grind the seeds into a coarse consistency and not into a powder.

Daikon Greens Miso Broth

PREPARATION TIME: 20 MINUTES
COOKING TIME: 8 MINUTES

This light and delicious broth is a great pick-me-up, as well as a fantastic meal if you are fighting a cold or the flu. It's a great substitute to a chicken soup!

I'm an avid consumer of dark leafy greens and would experiment with almost any edible greens to increase the variety and flavor of this amazing and powerful anti-inflammatory food.

Daikon greens are really fresh in the springtime and are powerhouse of nutrients. Daikon, like broccoli, belongs to the cruciferous family of vegetables and is a staple in Japanese cuisine.

Ingredients:
1 large bunch daikon greens, washed and
    roughly chopped
1 small red onion chopped (about 3
    tablespoons)
2 garlic cloves, peeled and grated
1 inch ginger, peeled and grated
1 small Thai chili, seeded and minced
    (optional)
1teaspoon extra virgin olive oil
½ teaspoon toasted sesame oil
1 tablespoon red miso (preferably organic),
    diluted in warm water
2 cups hot water
1 tablespoon lemon juice

1. Warm a heavy bottomed stainless steel soup pot for 45 seconds, then add the olive oil, swirling the pot around to coat the oil; add the chopped onions, garlic, ginger, and the Thai chili (if using) and sauté on high heat for 3 to 4 minutes.
2. Add the chopped greens and sauté for another 2 minutes, until the greens wilt. Remove the pot from heat.
3. Add the diluted miso, the hot water, and the toasted sesame oil. Cover the pot and let it sit for 5 to 10 minutes for the flavors to blend in before serving.

Note: I prefer grating garlic and ginger to chopping or mincing them, as I find it to be more flavorful and it blends better into the broth.

If you are planning on using the broth to ward off a cold, skip the toasted sesame oil and keep it light.

The reason for moving the soup pot to a cooler surface before adding the miso is to preserve the delicate live enzymes, as they are sensitive to direct heat.

Soba Noodle Soup

PREPARATION TIME: 15 TO 20 MINUTES
COOKING TIME: 6 MINUTES

Soba noodles are made from buckwheat and are super simple to prepare. They can be made in under 5 minutes. I like to cook the noodles al dente to avoid overcooked, limp noodles. However, feel free to cook the noodles the way you like them, or follow the directions on the package.

This is a spicy noodle soup in a Thai curry base. The addition of miso, ginger, and garlic makes this soup a rich soul food, and the veggies increase the goodness of this mouth-watering meal. Eat up!

Ingredients:
2 small bundles of soba noodles
½ red bell pepper, diced
1 cup green cabbage, diced
1 small bunch dino kale
1 teaspoon ginger, peeled and minced
5 large garlic cloves, peeled and minced
1 teaspoon Thai curry paste (red or green)
¾ tablespoon extra virgin olive oil
½ teaspoon virgin coconut oil
1 tablespoon barley miso paste, diluted in
    warm water
2 cups filtered water

Freshly ground black pepper to taste
Handful of fresh basil leaves
1 tablespoon of raw black sesame seeds,
  roughly pounded

1. Cook the soba noodles al dente or as directed in the package. Drain and set it aside.
2. Place a heavy bottomed stainless steel soup pot on medium heat; add the Thai curry paste and a small quantity of water about a tablespoon and dilute the paste. Now add the diced bell pepper, garlic, ginger, and the olive oil and sauté for 1 to 2 minutes; then add the cabbage and sauté for another 2 minutes.
3. Add the water and bring it to a quick boil. Turn off heat and move the soup pot to a cooler surface and add the diluted miso paste, freshly ground black pepper, basil leaves, cooked noodles, and the black sesame seeds. Give it a good stir, cover, and let sit for 5 to 10 minutes before serving.

Note: The reason for moving the soup pot to a cooler surface before adding the diluted miso paste is to preserve the delicate live enzymes, as they are sensitive to direct heat.

Zucchini Pinto Bean Soup

PREPARATION TIME: 10 TO 15 MINUTES
COOKING TIME: 9 TO 10 MINUTES

Once I learned about the hazardous health issues associated with canned tomatoes, I stopped using them. With canned tomatoes, it is not the tomatoes that are the problem, but the chemical commonly known as BPA that is used to coat the lining of the cans. BPA can leach into the food causing hormonal disruption, reproductive harm, and other risks. Sadly, children are more susceptible to the effects of this chemical. I admit, when I tried experimenting with fresh tomatoes versus canned, I was surprised to find that the canned version worked better, particularly for this soup. Then it dawned on me that the issue had to do with pre-cooked versus fresh tomatoes. So I started to pressure cook the tomatoes separately before incorporating them into the soup and it worked like a charm.

Ingredients:
1 medium zucchini, rinsed and sliced into
    quarter moons
1 small red onion, thinly sliced
1 tablespoon garlic, peeled and minced
¾ teaspoon dried thyme, crushed
½ teaspoon dried oregano
½ teaspoon red chili flakes (reduce quantity for
    a milder soup)
1 tablespoon extra virgin olive oil

3 medium ripe tomatoes, quartered

1 cup cooked pinto beans

½ cup frozen yellow sweet corn

1 bunch collard greens, rinsed and cut in thin ribbons

3 cups filtered water

1 tablespoon lemon juice

1. Pressure cook the tomatoes and set it aside.
2. Place a heavy bottom stainless steel soup pan or pot on medium heat. Add the oil and swirl it around to coat the base of the pan. After about 45 seconds, add the sliced onions, increase heat to high, and sauté for about 4 to 5 minutes.
3. Add the minced garlic, crushed herbs, red chili flakes, and the zucchini and continue sautéing for another minute.
4. Add the cooked tomatoes, collard greens, and the water. Bring to a rolling boil, add the cooked beans, reduce heat to low, cover, and cook the soup for about a minute.
5. Just as you are about to turn off the heat, add the frozen corn and the lemon juice. Stir well, cover, turn off heat, and let the soup sit on the stove for 10 minutes before serving.

Note: Make sure you crush the dried herbs before using to bring out their flavor. I use my fingers to crush the herbs and it works fine. You may also use a mortar and pestle.

Add more water if the soup is too thick, or you may enjoy it as a stew as well.

Tomato Tonic

I call this dish a tonic because I see it as an excellent invigorating drink, especially when feeling under the weather and you want to kickstart your day.

When I was growing up in India, cumin was regularly used both in my grandparents' and my mother's kitchens as a home remedy to help with indigestion and to fight a cold or flu. Thus, the cumin in this tonic is inspired by the amazing cooks with whom I grew up, who used ingredients not only to make food taste better, but to heal.

This tonic is super simple to prepare, especially if you have frozen cubed tomato puree or sauce.

Ingredients:
8 to 10 frozen cubed tomato sauce or 1 cup
    tomato puree
2 garlic cloves, peeled and smashed
1 teaspoon cumin seeds, broken (use mortar
    and pestle or spice grinder)
½ teaspoon mustard seeds (optional)
1 teaspoon extra virgin olive oil
1 tablespoon barley miso paste, diluted in warm
    water
1 ½ cup filtered water
Freshly cracked black pepper to taste

1. Place a heavy bottomed stainless steel soup pan on high heat and pop the mustard seeds, if you're using them.
2. Reduce heat to medium and add the oil and swirl the pan around to coat. Add the garlic, the broken cumin seeds, and the black pepper and sauté for 1 to 2 minutes, being mindful not to burn the spices.
3. Add the frozen tomato cubes or the tomato puree and the filtered water, bring it to rolling boil. Turn off heat and move the soup pot to a cooler surface.
4. Add the diluted miso paste, mix well, and let it sit for 5 minutes and serve with a slice of toasted whole grain bread. Simply heaven!

Note: In order to dilute the miso paste, add about 2 to 3 ounces of filtered water to one tablespoon of miso paste. Mix together.

You can skip using the mustard seeds if you like. I use it to give it an Indian feel, which is comforting to me. Moreover, the tiny seeds dotting the broth are really fun to look at. As the saying goes, we eat with our eyes first, so give it a try and see what you think!

Watercress Soup

PREPARATION TIME: 10 MINUTES
COOKING TIME: 5 MINUTES

Confession: I am not a fan of watercress. But it is an amazing superfood brimming with nutrients and compounds that may help prevent certain types of cancer.

I desperately tried to incorporate it into our lives without much luck, until I made it into a soup. The almond and cashew butters pleasantly mellow the sharp acrid flavor of the watercress, and garnishing it with sweet marjoram gives the soup a nice touch.

This soup is super simple and fast to prepare. Let the magic of cooking make you a fan of foods you once found distasteful so you can enjoy their health benefits! Enjoy!

Ingredients:
1 bunch watercress leaves and tender stem, rinsed and roughly chopped
1 tablespoon almond butter, diluted into paste
1 teaspoon cashew butter, diluted into paste
1 teaspoon ginger, peeled and grated
1 teaspoon lite Tamari sauce
¾ teaspoon red chili flakes (reduce quantity for a lite version)
1 tablespoon coconut milk
1 teaspoon freshly minced sweet marjoram
2 drops stevia (optional)
1½ cup filtered water

Juice of ½ small lime
Dash of freshly ground black pepper
Sea salt to taste (optional)

1. Place a heavy bottomed stainless steel soup pot on medium heat and add the diluted nut butters, ¼ cup of filtered water, red chili flakes, and ginger. Using a whisk, dilute the nut butters further into a rich paste.
2. Add the remaining water, increase heat to high, and as the mixture comes to a boil, reduce heat to medium-high. Add the chopped watercress and coconut milk. Cook for 1 to 2 minutes, until the watercress begins to wilt. Turn off heat, add lime juice and stevia (if using), mix well, and let it sit for 5 to 10 minutes before serving.

Hearty Black Bean Soup

PREPARATION TIME: 13 MINUTES
COOKING TIME: 9 MINUTES

The combination of minced garlic, sun dried tomatoes, and the abundant goodness of the black beans (bursting with high protein, fiber, and loaded with antioxidants) makes this soup one of my favorites.

Enjoy it with a slice of whole grain bread, or ladle a tablespoon or two of cooked whole grains to make this soup a wholesome meal.

Ingredients:
1 cup cooked black beans
3 large garlic cloves, peeled and minced
2 sun-dried tomatoes (soaked in oil), sliced into strips
1 tablespoon dried Italian herb blend, crushed
½ teaspoon red chili flakes
¼ cup tomato puree or 1 small tomato, minced
1 teaspoon virgin coconut oil
1½ cup green cabbage, roughly chopped
1 small bunch dino kale leaves, cut into ribbons
Freshly ground black pepper to taste
3 cups filtered water
2 tablespoons lime or lemon juice
Sea salt to taste

1. Place a heavy bottomed stainless steel soup pan on medium-low heat. Add the oil and swirl it around to coat the base of the pan. Add the garlic and sun-dried tomatoes, and sauté for a minute. Add the herbs, black pepper, red chili flakes, and sea salt, and continue sautéing for 30 seconds.
2. Now add the cabbage, increase heat to medium-high or high (depending on your stovetop) and sauté for 2 minutes. Add the tomato puree or the diced tomatoes, mix well, and continue sautéing for two minutes.
3. Add the black beans and kale. Mix well and sauté for a minute. Then add the water bring it to a rolling boil, reduce heat, cover, and cook the soup for 2 more minutes. Turn off heat, mix in the lime or lemon juice, and let the soup sit for at least 5 to 10 minutes before serving.

Note: For a spicier version of the soup, use generous amounts of black pepper and increase the quantity of chili flakes to one teaspoon. I personally enjoy the milder version of the soup (the original quantities) as it helps me savor the veggies. However, if you like spicy hot, go for it.

Dhal Soup

PREPARATION TIME: 10 MINUTES
COOKING TIME: 20 TO 30 MINUTES
SAUTÉING TIME: 4 MINUTES

The very first dish that I started to cook was lentils (dhal), mainly because it's super simple to prepare, nutritious, and really delicious. Also, I grew up eating dhal in one form or another almost every day, sometimes more than once a day.

If you're familiar with Indian food, then you know how essential dhal is to Indian cooking. Most westerners are not aware that each state in India (there are 29 of them) has a unique cooking method, way of combining spices, tempering the cooking oil, etc. The same dishes have completely different tastes depending on which part of India you visit. Hence the numerous ways to prepare dhal.

Dhal basically means lentils, and the commonly-used lentil in south India, especially Tamil Nadu (my native state), is thurvardhal, or thuvaramparuppu, as known in Tamil (the language spoken in Tamil Nadu and my mother tongue).

I use pink lentils to make my dhals. There is no need to soak these lentils overnight, but if you wish to soak them to reduce the phytic acid (to increase digestibility), by all means do so.

Pressuring cooking the lentils:

Ingredients for pressure cooker:
3 ounces pink lentils
4 cups filtered water (reduce water for a thicker consistency)
1 teaspoon turmeric powder
½ teaspoon asafetida
½ teaspoon red chili powder
Sea salt to taste

1. Rinse the lentils well before placing them in the cooker. Add water, spices, and sea salt. Cover the cooker.
2. Pressure cook for 12 minutes after three whistles.

Ingredients for tempering:
1 teaspoon black mustard seeds
½ teaspoon cumin seeds
1 dried red chili, broken into 2 or 3 pieces
   (discard seeds for less heat)
1 teaspoon organic virgin coconut oil or
   avocado oil
Handful of cilantro leaves (optional)

1. Place a small stainless steel or cast iron skillet on high heat. Add the mustard seeds to the skillet and the moment the seeds begin to pop, add the cumin seeds and the broken chili pieces (if using). Reduce heat to low, and with a help of wooden spoon, move the seeds around continuously for about 30 seconds or less. Remove from heat. Add the oil and set it aside.

2. Once it is safe to open the pressure cooker, mix in the tempered seeds-oil mixture and add the cilantro leaves (if using) into the cooked lentils and serve.

Note: Although pressure cooking the lentils saves considerable time, if you prefer to cook the lentils in a regular soup pot, see method below.

1. Place the rinsed lentil in a soup pot, add water, turmeric, and asafetida, and bring it to a rolling boil.

2. Reduce heat to medium-low or simmer (depending upon your stovetop), cover the pot, and cook for 20 to 30 minutes, or until the lentils are soft. To know that they are soft, see if they mash easily by pressing a few against a wooden cutting board with a spoon.

Grains, Pasta, & Noodles

Millet Upma

I grew up eating a savory dish called "upma" either for breakfast or as an evening teatime snack, commonly referred to as "tiffin time" in Indian English.

Traditionally, upma is made from semolina, which is a cracked, refined wheat product. The closest equivalent is couscous.

Since refined wheat products are a no-no in my kitchen, I tried experimenting with millet, and the outcome was just as good. I hope you enjoy it as much as we do!

Ingredients for cooking millet:
¾ cup millet, rinsed well
2 cups filtered water
¼ teaspoon asafetida powder
¼ teaspoon turmeric powder
¼ teaspoon red chili powder
¼ teaspoon extra virgin olive oil
Sea salt to taste

Bring the 2 cups of water to boil in a non-reactive pot and add the remaining ingredients. Stir well and bring the mixture to a rolling boil. Reduce heat to simmer, cover the pot, and cook the millet for 20 to 30 minutes until the millet is well done but not mushy. Remove from heat. With the help of a wooden fork, fluff the millet, breaking any lumps. Cover and set it aside.

Ingredients for seasoning:
¼ teaspoon asafetida powder
¼ teaspoon turmeric powder
1 teaspoon black mustard seeds
1 teaspoon cumin seeds
½ small red onion, diced
7 stalks of green onion (only the green part),
    thinly sliced
2 tablespoon cilantro leaves, minced
1-inch piece of ginger, peeled and minced
1 tablespoon virgin coconut oil or avocado oil
1 tablespoon raw cashew nuts, roughly chopped

1. Place a sauté pan on high heat and pop the mustard seeds. As they begin to pop, remove the pan from heat and swirl the pan for even distribution of heat. Place the pan back on heat and add the cumin seeds. As the cumin seeds begin to toast, giving out a spicy aroma, around 20 seconds or so, remove the pan from heat and set it aside.

2. In another sauté pan, gently warm the oil under low heat for 30 seconds. Add the red and green onions, increase heat to medium-high, and continue sautéing for a minute or so. Add a teaspoon of water to avoid burning the onions or sticking them to the pan. Add the popped mustard and the toasted cumin seeds, chopped ginger, and the spices, and continue sautéing for 2 to 3 minutes. Add a teaspoon of water if the onions stick to the pan. Remove from heat. Mix in the sautéed onions and the cashew nuts into the cooked millet and stir well, break any lumps with a wooden fork, and serve.

Notes: It is easier to fluff and break down lumps as the millet cools down. Avoid using a regular spoon to fluff the millet as it tends to make the millet mushy.

I prefer well-cooked millet instead of cooking it al dente, not only because it is better for digestion, but also because the spices are better integrated.

Pistachio Pilaf

PREPARATION TIME: 10 MINUTES
COOKING TIME: 51 MINUTES

This is a great, festive dish, studded with nuts and dried fruits and meant to be a party pleaser! Freshly cooked rice makes all the difference. I like to prepare this dish a few hours prior and warm it just before serving. You can also prepare this dish a day in advance, cool it down to room temperature, store it an airtight container in the fridge, and warm it the next day before serving.

> ### Ingredients for cooking rice:
> ½ cup brown Basmati rice, rinsed well
> 1¼ cups filtered water or veggie broth
> ½ teaspoon extra virgin olive oil

In a heavy bottomed pan, gently warm the oil on medium heat for about a minute or so. Add the rinsed rice and sauté it for 3 to 4 minutes, stirring continuously. Add the water or broth and increase heat to high. Bring the liquid to a boil, reduce heat to simmer, cover the pan, and cook the rice for 30 to 40 minutes, or until the rice is done.

Note: Do not stir or uncover the rice during the cooking time.

Ingredients for sautéing:
1 tablespoon virgin coconut oil or avocado oil
1 small red onion, diced
1 inch cinnamon stick, broken into small pieces
2 whole cloves
¾ teaspoon turmeric powder
¾ teaspoon red chili powder
¾ teaspoon fennel powder
¾ teaspoon paprika powder
¾ cup unsweetened almond milk or milk of
    your choice
¼ cup raw pistachios, minced
¼ cup raw walnuts, minced
2 tablespoons raisins
Sea salt to taste
2 to 3 strands of saffron for garnishing

1. Place a large skillet on low heat and gently warm the oil. Add the cinnamon sticks and cloves, increase heat to medium-high, and sauté for 30 seconds. Add the remaining spices and continue sautéing for a minute, until the spices release a fragrant aroma. To avoid burning the spices, adjust the heat if necessary and continue stirring.

2. Add the diced onions, increase heat to high, and sauté for 3 to 4 minutes. To avoid burning the onions, sprinkle small amounts of water and continue sautéing on high heat.

3. Add the minced nuts, raisins, milk, and salt. Bring it to a quick boil. Reduce heat to simmer, cover, and cook for 3 to 5 minutes. Turn off heat.

4. Once the rice is cooked, using a wooden or regular fork, fluff the rice and combine it with the onion mixture. If any liquid remains after the rice is done, increase heat and let the liquid evaporate. Be mindful not to burn the rice. Remove from stovetop, stir in the saffron strands, and serve.

Soothing Rice

PREPARATION TIME: 5 MINUTES

This recipe gets its name from the following story: Three decades ago, I was the youngest resident at Bede Griffiths' idyllic ashram in S. India, when I developed a deep dry hacking cough that lasted for several weeks and would simply not go away. Sister Stephanie, a beautiful Indian nun and a resident at the ashram (during this time, she had taken a vow of silence for a period of five years), came to my rescue. She had studied yoga and Hindu philosophy with Swami Sivananda in the foothills of the Himalayas, and was quite steeped in natural healing.

At noon every day, just before the temple bell rang for the mid-day prayer, Sr. Stephanie would faithfully and silently appear at my hut with a plate of hot steaming rice and lovingly nursed me back to health.

Sr. Stephanie's remedy was very simple: hot cooked rice mixed with sesame oil and sprinkled with specks of freshly ground black pepper, then made into small balls. The key was to swallow the balls of rice as hot as one could. When the heat from the steaming rice hit the throat, it was soothing, and to my amazement, it worked like a charm.

For the past 21 years, we have and continue to take a group of people from the West on our annual life-transforming pilgrimage and retreat to this very special and one of a kind ashram (based in S. India), which is our spiritual home to this date.

Ingredients:
1 cup cooked brown rice
½ teaspoon toasted sesame oil
½ teaspoon red chili pepper flakes
1 tablespoon unhulled sesame seeds,
    coarsely pounded
Sea salt to taste

Make sure that the rice is nice and hot. Add the oil, red chili pepper flakes, sea salt, and the pounded sesame seeds, mix well with the help of a wooden fork and serve piping hot. If you enjoyed the story, you might want to round them into balls.

Notes: Using a fork instead of spoon helps to keep the rice nice and fluffy, without turning it into a gooey mush.

To pound the sesame seeds, use a mortar and pestle or a spice grinder.

Aromatic Quinoa

PREPARATION TIME: 15 MINUTES
COOKING TIME: 15 MINUTES

This is a simple and delicious way of preparing quinoa. The spices impart an exotic flavor as they penetrate and infuse this supergrain. The onions and the ginger add an extra zing. Make a large batch and save it for two or more meals. It actually tastes better the next day, as the spices have had time to work their magic. If you plan on keeping it for an extra day or two, be sure to refrigerate it in an airtight container.

Ingredients for pressure cooking the quinoa:
½ **cup red quinoa**
¼ **cup white quinoa**
1 **teaspoon extra virgin olive oil**
⅛ **teaspoon all spice**
¼ **teaspoon cardamom powder**
½ **teaspoon turmeric powder**
¾ **teaspoon red chili flakes (reduce quantity for less heat)**
2 **drops stevia**
2 **cups filtered water**
Sea salt to taste

Place the rinsed and drained quinoa in the pressure cooker, add the ingredients listed for pressure cooking, and cook for 11 minutes.

Ingredients for sautéing:
½ small red onion, diced
¼ teaspoon ginger, peeled and minced
1 Thai green chili, seeded and minced
    (optional)
1 tablespoon cilantro leaves, minced
1 tablespoon virgin coconut oil or avocado oil

1. Place a skillet on medium heat and add the onions and oil. Stir well to coat the onions with oil. Increase heat to high and sauté for 3 to 4 minutes until the onions turn golden. Add the minced ginger and the cilantro and continue sautéing for another minute or two. Reduce heat if necessary to avoid burning the onions. Turn off heat.
2. When the quinoa is done and it is safe to open the pressure cooker, fold the onion mixture into the cooked quinoa and serve.

Garlicky Capellini

PREPARATION TIME: 20 MINUTES
COOKING TIME: 16 MINUTES

Whole wheat capellini (very similar to angel hair pasta, but slightly thicker) is a delightful blessing for pasta lovers like me who can indulge in it from time to time without feeling guilty. However, as always, moderation is the key to life, which reminds me of Oscar Wilde's quote: *"Everything in moderation, including moderation."*

This is a very simple dish to prepare. The only time-consuming part is the garlic peeling and mincing. You may use pre-minced garlic (available in most supermarkets), but if you have the time and the inclination, there's nothing quite like using freshly minced garlic. It makes all the difference.

Ingredients for cooking the pasta:
10 ounces whole wheat capellini pasta
1 ½ tablespoons extra virgin olive oil
Sea Salt to taste
½ teaspoon red chili flakes

1. Bring a large pot of water to boil. Salt the water (optional). Add ½ teaspoon of extra virgin olive oil to the boiling water. Add the pasta and cook al dente.
   Drain the pasta into a colander, rinse well with filtered water to remove stickiness, and drain the water.
2. Place the drained pasta in a large bowl and add one tablespoon of extra virgin olive and the red chili flakes.

Toss with a wooden fork and cover the bowl partially to prevent the pasta from becoming dry. Set aside.

Ingredients for sautéing:
1 large bunch of dinosaur kale (just the leaves), washed and cut into thin ribbons
2 large heads of garlic, peeled and minced
3 to 4 whole red chili (stems removed)
½ teaspoon red chili pepper flakes (optional)
¼ teaspoon freshly ground black pepper
4 slices of sun-dried tomatoes soaked in oil, thinly sliced
1 tablespoon extra virgin olive oil
Sea salt to taste

1. Place a large skillet on medium heat and warm the skillet for 45 seconds. Add the oil and swirl the skillet around to coat it with the oil. Add minced garlic, whole red chilies, chili pepper flakes (if using), sun-dried tomatoes, and sauté on high heat for about a minute. Reduce heat if necessary to avoid burning the garlic.
2. Add the kale, sea salt, and black pepper. Increase heat slowly to high and sauté for 2 to 3 minutes.
3. Turn off heat and move the skillet to a cooler surface to avoid further cooking the kale. Add the cooked pasta, mix well, and serve.

Notes: The amount of garlic you add determines the flavor of this dish. My husband Russill does not like the flavor of raw garlic, but he loves it sautéed.

The use of the whole red chili is mainly to add color and make the dish look exotic. As long as you keep the chili whole, without breaking it, it will not release any heat/spiciness.

Japanese Noodles with Pepitas

PREPARATION TIME: 15 MINUTES
COOKING TIME: 5 MINUTES

Pepitas is the Mexican term for pumpkin seeds, which are packed with iron and zinc. Japanese soba noodles are made out of buckwheat flour, another nutritional powerhouse, and naturally gluten free. Together, they make a rich combination of protein and fiber.

Enjoy this noodle dish for breakfast, especially on a cold winter morning, or as an entrée for lunch or dinner.

Ingredients:
1 cup cooked soba noodles
¼ cup raw pumpkin seeds
½ teaspoon red chili flakes
1 clove of garlic, peeled
Sea salt to taste
1 tablespoon extra virgin olive oil

1. Place the pumpkin seeds, chili flakes, garlic, and sea salt in a stone or wooden mortar and pound until the garlic is smashed and the pumpkin seeds are broken into small pieces.

2. To warm the pre-cooked noodles, place them in a nonreactive dish, added boiling hot filtered water, and let them sit for a minute. Drain the noodles by pouring them into a wire mesh. Shake the noodles to remove any excess water.

   If you do not have leftover cooked noodles, then prepare the noodles as per the directions on the packet. Drain well and set aside.
3. Warm the oil in a skillet on medium heat for about 30 seconds. Remove the skillet from heat. Add the pounded pumpkin seeds to the warmed oil and mix well. Now add the soba noodles (make sure the noodles are warm and drained well) to the skillet, toss, and serve.

Street Noddles

PREPARATION TIME: 25 MINUTES
COOKING TIME: 9 MINUTES

Growing up in India, street food was always plentiful, either in the form of snacks or as a complete meal. The aroma and the tantalizing energy surrounding these street vendors in the evening twilight as the hot tropical sun disappeared was simply magical.

Partaking in food from a street stall was a very special treat rarely permitted in our household, as my parents were perpetually worried that the oil and water used for cooking were not up to par. So when permitted (this happened mainly during summer holidays) my siblings and I were ecstatic and made good use of the opportunity. One of my favorite treats was an Indian styled Hakka veg noodles—a Chinese noodle dish made from wheat flour, veggies, and lots of spices.

This recipe is inspired by my love for Hakka noodles, but a healthier version. The use of mung bean noodles (also known as bean thread or cellophane noodles) makes this dish completely grain- and gluten-free, which is really nice if you are in the mood for eating noodles.

Ingredients:

8 ounces mungbeannoodles

1 cup red onion, chopped

1 cup green cabbage, roughly chopped

1 small red bell pepper, diced

1 bunch dino kale, sliced into ribbons

½ cup broccoli florets

1 tablespoon Thai red curry paste (reduce quantity for a milder version)

2½ tablespoons extra virgin olive oil

¼ teaspoon red chili flakes (optional)

1 tablespoon lite tamari sauce

Handful of cilantro leaves with the stem attached

1. Place the bean thread noodles in a non-reactive pot and pour hot boiling water over the noodles. Cover the pot and let it sit for 3 minutes. Drain the noodles well and rinse in cold water. Place the noodles on a cutting board and chop them roughly, then set aside. Giving the noodles a rough chop will help them mix better with the cooked veggies, but you don't have to.

2. In a large skillet place the Thai curry paste and dilute it with 1 or 2 tablespoon of filtered water. Place the skillet on medium heat and add the chopped onions and 1½ tablespoon of oil. Increase heat to medium-high and sauté the onions for about 3 minutes; sprinkle a small quantity of water while sautéing if necessary to avoid burning the onions.

3. Add the cabbage and the red bell pepper give it a good stir. Cover the skillet and cook on medium heat for about 2 minutes.

4. Add the kale, stir well, cover and cook for another 2 minutes.
5. Add the cilantro leaves with the stem, sauté for 1 minute.
6. Turn off heat and move the skillet to a cooler surface, add the noodles, tamari sauce, and the remaining oil, toss well and serve.

Note: Unlike regular sautéing where you cook by uncovering the skillet on high heat, I use the technique of covering the skillet because it helps cook the veggies faster and more evenly with the steam induced by covering the skillet. You need to keep a close watch. The best thing to do is use a timer so that you don't overcook the veggies. Also, the right amount of heat— medium to medium-high—depends on your stovetop, and plays a crucial role in not overcooking or burning the veggies. This is a super simple and easy method, once you get the hang of it.

Vegetables

Buttered Green Beans

PREPARATION TIME: 15 MINUTES
COOKING TIME: 6 MINUTES

When I was about eleven or so, my mother occasionally delegated to me the errand of shopping for vegetables. I did not receive a lot of compliments from her when it came to domestic skills or virtues, so I was quite elated when she said that I had a good eye for choosing fresh, tender vegetables, better than my sister, who loved helping my mother in the kitchen and who, from a very young age, turned out to be a remarkable cook.

Proud to be entrusted with such an important errand, I would set off on my blue Atlas bicycle to bring home my favorite vegetable: tender, succulent green beans. "Is this all they had?" she would tease me and nod approvingly of the beans. And I would feel deeply gratified at having accomplished a grown-up chore done to perfection. To this day, I love green beans, although I do not prepare them the way my mom does. Her preparation is labor intensive. I have found my own way to enjoy them without too much effort.

The recipe below is a fun and delicious way to prepare green beans and can be done in a matter of minutes. The pecans add a distinct flavor. We love eating it as a mid-afternoon or late evening snack. And it is just as good as a side dish, especially for a festive occasion, like Thanksgiving.

Ingredients:
½ pound tender green beans, stalk ends
    removed
¼ cup raw pecans, chopped
¾ teaspoon almond butter
¼ teaspoon cashew butter
¼ teaspoon red chili flakes
Freshly ground black pepper to taste
Sea salt to taste
1 ½ teaspoon lemon juice
½ teaspoon extra virgin olive oil

1. Bring a large pot of water to a rolling boil. Salt it, if you desire, and add the green beans. Cook the beans for 4 minutes. Once the green beans are cooked, drain the beans and set it aside.
2. In the meantime, prepare the dressing. In a large glass bowl, add 3 tablespoons of the cooking water from the beans, lemon juice, almond and cashew butter, and whisk the mixture well and set it aside.
3. Place a large skillet on medium heat for about 45 seconds. Add the oil and coat the surface of the pan with oil. Add the chili flakes, the well-drained green beans, and the chopped pecans; sauté for 1 minute. Turn off heat and move the pan to a cooler surface.
4. Pour the almond-cashew butter dressing over the beans, toss well, and serve.

Isabel's Cabbage

PREPARATION TIME: 5 MINUTES
COOKING TIME: 4 MINUTES

The first time I tasted this dish was in my dear Aunt Isabel's house in India. I was surprised by how simple and easy it was to prepare. Isabel's cooking repertoire was very limited, but she was exceptionally proud of this dish, and rightfully so. She was also the first person to introduce me to natural healing and so this dish carries her name.

Spas were a novelty in India in the late 1980s. Isabel frequented spas to cleanse and rejuvenate. This dish is so special to me because my aunt was so supportive, compassionate, and caring not just to me, but to almost anyone she happened to meet. Everyone in our family adored her. This soft, buttery dish captures her personality rather well.

I prefer to steam the cabbage rather than boiling or sautéing. Moreover, please note that the butter is not heated. Try experimenting with savoy or purple cabbage, in addition to green, and see what works best for you.

Ingredients
1½ cup green cabbage, roughly chopped into
    bite size pieces
1 teaspoon grass-fed pasture-raised butter
Freshly ground black pepper to taste
¼ teaspoon red chili flakes (optional)
Sea salt to taste

1. Steam the cabbage for about three to four minutes, until tender but not limp.
2. Once the cabbage is cooked, shake off any excess water, pat dry if necessary, and place in a glass container. Add the grass-fed pasture-raised butter, red chili flakes (if using them), freshly ground black pepper, and sea salt.
3. Cover the container with a spill-proof lid and shake vigorously for about 20 to 30 seconds and serve immediately.

Ribbon Kale In Almond Cashew Sauce

PREPARATION TIME: 7 MINUTES
COOKING TIME: 3 MINUTES

In our household, we eat kale at least two to three times a week. It is a staple in my refrigerator. This recipe is super simple, delicious, and fast to prepare, so there is no excuse to avoid eating your greens!

The nut butters, apart from being a rich source of protein and antioxidants, makes this dish absolutely delicious, and the kale of course is a nutritional powerhouse.

Ingredients:
1 large bunch of green or purple kale
1 tablespoon almond butter
1 tablespoon walnut or cashew butter
2 tablespoons lemon juice
¼ teaspoon red chili flakes
1 drop stevia (optional)
Sea salt to taste

1. Remove the kale leaves from the stems. Reserve the stems for stocks or soups if you like, or you may compost them. Rinse the leaves well, drain until dry, and cut them into thin strips of ribbon. Steam the kale for 3 minutes.
2. Place the nut butters in a large bowl, then add 3 tablespoons of the hot water that was used to steam the kale, lemon juice, red chili flakes, and the stevia (if using), and whisk briskly to dilute the butter.
3. Add the steamed kale to the butter mixture, toss well, and serve.

Note: It is easier to dilute nut butters with hot water rather than room temperature water. I like to use the water left over from steaming the kale for the added nutritional benefit.

I like using raw nut butters compared to roasted.

Basil Flavored Cabbage & Kale

PREPARATION TIME: 13 MINUTES
COOKING TIME: 7 MINUTES

I often pair veggies together to enhance their flavors, and one such favorite combination is cabbage and kale. This dish is simply spiced with black pepper, which augments the natural taste of these super veggies. The touch of basil leaves and toasted sesame oil gives it an Asian feel. Enjoy!

Ingredients:
1 cup green cabbage, thinly sliced but not too
   fine
1 small red bell pepper, thinly sliced
1 bunch dino kale, rinsed, drained, and sliced
   into thin ribbons
2 tablespoons filtered water
1 teaspoon extra virgin olive oil
Freshly ground pepper to taste
Sea salt to taste
½ teaspoon toasted sesame oil
10 to 12 large fresh basil leaves, thinly sliced

1. Place a large skillet on low heat and warm the oil for 30 seconds. Increase heat to medium-high, and add the sliced red bell pepper and sauté for a minute.
2. Add the sliced cabbage, kale, black pepper, and sea salt to taste, and continue sautéing for another 30 seconds. Sprinkle small amounts of filtered water from time to time and sauté for about 4 minutes, until veggies turn bright colors.
3. Just as you are ready to turn off the heat, stir in the basil leaves and the toasted sesame oil, mix well, remove from heat, and serve piping hot.

Note: The sprinkling of small amounts of water from time to time (a teaspoon or so at a time) helps to avoid burning the veggies. However, be mindful not to add too much water, as the dish will become soggy and insipid.

Golden Coconut-Laced Cauliflower

This is my mother's recipe, given to me over international phone lines. When I need inspiration to make a traditional Indian dish, I call my mother or my sister and they generously offer their suggestions with incredible passion and gusto. Both of them are excellent cooks, each with their own unique style, and they demonstrate their love through the medium of cooking, even more so than words.

To this day, I feel a deep sense of comfort and joy eating their homemade dishes when I hang out with them in India after our annual pilgrimage. As they lovingly prepare fresh hot adais (recipe towards the end) or chapattis, they share stories about our extended family, antics, and dramas!

This is a very simple dish to prepare. The main spice used is turmeric powder, which gives the cauliflower the golden hue, and adds antioxidant goodness. The asafetida powder not only gives an Indian flavor, but it is known for its anti-gas properties (cauliflower, despite its extraordinary nutritional value, tends to produce flatulence) and is known to aid overall digestion. The final touch of coconut flakes makes this dish utterly yummy, same as mummy's!

Ingredients:
1 large cauliflower, cut into small pieces
1 teaspoon mustard seeds
1 tablespoon yellow split peas
½ teaspoon red chili flakes (optional)
1 teaspoon turmeric powder
¼ teaspoon asafetida powder
¾ tablespoon virgin coconut oil or
    extra virgin olive oil
Freshly ground black pepper to taste
2 tablespoons coconut flakes
Sea salt to taste

1. Place a large skillet on high heat and pop the mustard seeds. As the seeds begin to pop, add the yellow spilt peas, reduce heat to low, and with the help of a wooden spoon or spatula, dry roast the peas for 45 seconds. Turn off the heat and move the skillet to a cooler surface to avoid burning.
2. Add the spices and mix them into the popped mustard seeds and roasted peas. Add the cauliflower and oil, and mix well.
3. Place the skillet back on high heat, sprinkle about a tablespoon of filtered water, and sauté the veggies for about a minute. Be mindful to avoid burning them. Lower the heat to medium-low, cover and cook the cauliflower for about 5 minutes.
4. Move the skillet to a cooler surface to avoid further cooking the veggies, sprinkle the coconut flakes, mix well, and serve.

Baked Tomatoes

Tomatoes and sautéed garlic are a match made in heaven. Your taste buds and your immune system will thank you for this combination. This is a great party dish; you can prepare the tomatoes and the garlic oil in advance and bake the tomatoes 20 minutes before serving.

Ingredients:
3 ripe tomatoes, washed, cored, and halved
8 cloves of garlic, peeled and grated
1 teaspoon red pepper flakes (reduce quantity
    for a milder version)
2 tablespoons extra virgin olive oil
1 tablespoon virgin coconut oil or avocado oil
2 tablespoons thinly sliced fresh basil leaves
Freshly ground black pepper
Sea salt

1. Generously sprinkle the halved tomatoes with freshly ground black pepper and sea salt to taste and set aside.
2. Grease a large rectangular non-reactive baking dish with virgin coconut oil or avocado oil. Place the tomatoes cut side down on the greased dish and bake the tomatoes uncovered at 375° F for about 10 to 15 minutes.
3. Place a medium-sized skillet on high heat for 1 minute. Add the olive oil and swirl the pan around to coat its surface. Reduce the heat to medium-high, add the grated garlic and the red pepper flakes, and sauté for about 30 to 45 seconds. Reduce the heat to low and let the garlic simmer for 2 to 3 minutes. Since the garlic can easily burn, pay close attention. Add the basil leaves, and continue cooking for about 30 seconds. Turn off the heat, and move the garlic oil to a cooler surface.
4. Place the baked tomatoes (cut side up) on the serving plates and spoon the garlic oil over the tomatoes and serve.

Swiss Chard & Olives

I created this recipe more out of necessity than by choice, since all I had left in my refrigerator was a bunch of chard and a couple of carrots. Yes, it was time to go shopping, but I have learnt not to shop on an empty stomach, for that is when I am most likely to eat out and least likely to choose wisely. I wasn't sure how this dish was going to turn out, but the olives in the pantry came to the rescue and to my happy surprise, it was a winner.

Ingredients:
8 to 10 pimiento-stuffed green olives, quartered
1 large carrot, scrubbed and dice
1 large bunch Swiss chard, washed
1 tablespoon extra virgin olive oil
¾ teaspoon red chili flakes (reduce quantity for less heat)
Freshly ground black pepper to taste (optional)
Sea salt to taste

1. Bring a large pot of water to a rolling boil.
2. Prepare the chard by cutting and discarding the tough stems while keeping the part of the stems that are tender.
3. Add the chard to the boiling water and cook for 3 minutes. Drain the cooked chard in a colander and let it cool. Squeeze out the remaining water from the chard, give it a rough chop, and set it aside.
4. Place a large skillet on medium heat for about 30 to 45 seconds. Add the oil and swirl the skillet to coat it with oil. Add the red chili flakes, diced carrots, and olives, and sauté on medium-high heat for about 2 to 3 minutes. If necessary, sprinkle small amounts of water to avoid burning, and continue sautéing.
5. Add the chard to the carrots and olives, mix well, remove from heat, and serve.

Note: To save time, I usually boil the chard half an hour or so before preparing the carrots for sautéing. This way, I don't have to wait for the chard to cool before handling it. You can always place the chard in an ice bath to cool it faster.

Beans

Black Bean Tacos

This is great lunch dish, quick and easy to prepare, especially if you have leftover cooked black beans. Of course, you can always open a can of beans if you are in a hurry. My choice is to avoid using canned foods as much as possible due to BPA (Bisphenol-A) and other toxic chemicals leaching into the food.

Pressure cooking your beans is easy, fast, and a healthier option. I usually pressure cook a large batch of beans that will last for at least two to three meals. Pre-cooked beans keep very well for at least three days when stored in airtight containers and refrigerated.

Ingredients:
1 cup cooked black beans
4 organic corn tortillas
4 tablespoons organic grass-fed raw cheddar cheese (or nut butter cheese)
3 tablespoons green onions, chopped
1 tablespoon cilantro leaves, minced
1 medium tomato, diced
4 leaves of romaine lettuce, shredded
Small quantity of microgreens
1 Thai chili, seeded and chopped (optional)
1 tablespoon lime juice
1 teaspoon organic virgin coconut oil
Freshly ground black pepper (optional)
Sea salt to taste

1. Place sauté pan on medium heat and add chili (if using), black beans, and the coconut oil and cook for about 3 minutes. Now add the cilantro leaves and cook for another 2 minutes. Turn off heat, add the lime juice, mix well, and set aside.
2. Sprinkle the diced tomatoes with freshly ground black pepper and sea salt. You can skip the black pepper for a milder version.
3. Warm the tortilla on a cast iron skillet, top it with black beans, shredded lettuce, diced tomato, chopped green onions, sprinkle the cheese, and serve.

Note: Please be mindful when you use dairy alternatives for cheese, as most of the so-called "healthy" cheese alternatives invariably contain ingredients that are unhealthy.

Spicy Red Beans

This is a really delicious and simple way to prepare beans. Feel free to substitute kidney beans instead of using red beans, as they are both equally nutritious.

The dish tastes better the next day, as the spices have had time to blend well and work their magic. I usually make enough to last a couple of meals.

Chana masala and the pavbhaji masala (both are popular northern Indian spice mixtures) can be easily purchased from any Indian grocery store. The brand that I like to use is Achi . If you cannot get this brand, choose any other, but make sure there are no artificial colors or additives in the spice powders.

Pressuring cooking the beans:

PREPARATION TIME: 5 MINUTES
PRESSURING COOKING TIME: 10 MINUTES

1 cup red beans, soaked overnight
¾ teaspoon turmeric powder
Filtered water
½ teaspoon asafoetida powder
Sea salt to taste

1. Rinse the beans well, add the spices, cover the beans with enough filtered water, but not beyond the halfway mark, and pressure cook the beans for 10 minutes.

2. Once the cooker has cooled down and it is safe to open, pour the cooked beans into a colander, rinse well, shake of the excess water, and set aside.

   If cooking the beans in a regular soup pot, add all the ingredients and bring it to a boil, reduce heat to medium, cover the pot and cook for about 30 to 40 minutes, or until the beans are done but firm. Once cooked, pour the beans into a colander, rinse well, shake of the excess water, and set aside.

SAUCE PREPARATION TIME: 13 MINUTES
SAUCE COOKING TIME: 21MINUTES

Ingredients for Sauce:
1 large yellow onion, chopped
3 small tomatoes, chopped
1 teaspoon chana masala powder
1 teaspoon pavbhaji masala powder
2 tablespoons lemon juice
1 tablespoon virgin coconut oil or avocado oil

1. Place a heavy bottomed soup pot on medium-high heat, add the onions and oil, and sauté for about 3 to 4 minutes, until the onions begin to brown.
2. Add the tomatoes and continue sautéing for another 2 minutes on high heat. Now add the spices powders, the cooked beans, and ½ cup of water. Mix well, increase heat to high and bring it to a boil, reduce heat to medium-low or simmer (depending on your stovetop), cover the pot, and cook for 15 minutes. Turn off heat, add the lemon juice, mix well, and let the sauce sit at least for 15 minutes before serving.

Note: The sauce should have a nice, thick consistency like a stew. If the sauce retains too much water, uncover the pot, increase heat to medium-high, and let the excess water evaporate. Stir it from time to time to avoid burning.

I prefer well-cooked beans for easier digestion, hence the pressuring cooking time is 10 minutes. For firmer beans, reduce time by a minute or 2.

If you are using kidney beans instead of red beans, increase the pressure cooking time to 20 minutes and if cooking it on stove top to 45 minutes to an hour.

Chickpea Curry

The word curry, especially in Western countries, conjures up images of colorful and rich Indian dishes, mainly sauces. However, the word curry in Tamil, the language I grew up with (in India) refers to vegetables, as in "kaikari." It could also mean meat as in "kolikari" (chicken meat).

In keeping with Western notions, this recipe is a mildly flavored sauce, with the exception of green chili. You can skip the chili for an even milder version.

Pressuring cooking the chickpeas:
Preparation Time: 5 minutes
Pressuring Cooking Time: 15minutes
1 cup of dried chickpeas, soaked overnight
¾ teaspoon turmeric powder
½ teaspoon asafoetida powder
Filtered water
Sea salt to taste

1. Rinse the chickpeas well, add the spices, cover it with enough filtered water, but not beyond the halfway mark. Pressure cook the chickpeas for 15 minutes.
2. Once the cooker has cooled down and it is safe to open, pour the cooked chickpea into a colander, rinse well, shake of the excess water, and set it aside.

    If cooking the chickpeas on a regular soup pot, add all the ingredients and bring it to a boil, reduce heat to medium, cover the pot, and cook for about an hour to an hour and a half, or until the chickpeas are done but firm. Once cooked, pour the chickpeas into a colander, rinse well, shake of the excess water, and set aside.

SAUCE PREPARATION TIME: 10 MINUTES
SAUCE COOKING TIME: 9 MINUTES

Ingredients for the Sauce:
1 small red onion, thinly sliced
1 large garlic clove, peeled and grated
½ teaspoon ginger, peeled and grated
2 medium tomatoes, chopped
2 tablespoons tomato puree (optional)
1 green Thai chili, seeded and thinly sliced
1 tablespoon virgin coconut oil or avocado oil
2 teaspoons coriander seeds, dry roasted and powdered
¾ teaspoon cumin, dry roasted and powdered
½ teaspoon turmeric powder
1 cup filtered water
2 tablespoons lemon juice
Sea salt to taste

1. Place a saucepan on medium heat, add the sliced onions and the oil, and sauté for about 3 to 4 minutes, until the onions begin to turn transparent.
3. Add the chopped tomatoes, ginger, garlic, chili, and the spices, and continue sautéing for another 2 minutes.
4. Add the cooked chickpeas and the filtered water, increase heat to high, and bring it to a boil. Turn off the heat, add the lemon juice, mix well, cover the pot, and let it sit for at least 10 to 15 minutes before serving.

Spinach Hummus
(A Hip Dip)

This is a cool dish that you can use as a dip for veggies, as a spread for wraps, or even as soup! If you are inclined to use it as a soup, dilute the consistency and enjoy with a small salad.

I like using a large quantity of spinach, which not only imparts a vibrant color, but more importantly, Popeye would approve!

The addition of cilantro gives the hummus (or soup) a nice herbal effect. Giving the cilantro leaves a quick hot bath helps dispel the soapy taste. If you still prefer not to use cilantro, you may substitute Italian flat leaf parsley or basil leaves.

Ingredients:
1½ cups cooked chickpeas beans
16 ounces baby spinach, rinsed and excess water shaken
A large handful of cilantro leaves
¾ teaspoon garlic powder
½ teaspoon red chili flakes
2 tablespoons tahini (preferably raw)
Freshly ground black pepper to taste
Juice of 1 small lemon
1 cup hot water
1 tablespoon extra virgin olive oil (optional)

1. Place the rinsed cilantro in a large colander and set in the sink.
2. Bring a large pot of water to a rolling boil.
3. Set the timer to a minute, add the rinsed spinach to the boiling water, and after a minute, drain the spinach in the colander over the cilantro leaves and shake off the excess water.
4. Place the cooked chickpeas, cooked spinach-cilantro, and all the remaining ingredients in a blender or food processor and blend into a smooth creamy puree.

Note: This hummus keeps well for a day or two in the refrigerator. If you plan to refrigerate it, remember to cool the hummus to a room temperature before doing so.

Lentil Stew

This delicately flavored stew is an all-time favorite of Russill's. Adding a handful of barley makes it a complete meal. I use unhulled barley instead of polished or pearled barley. It takes longer to cook, but once you soak the barley overnight or for the matter even for a few hours it reduces the cooking time. Moreover, if you are planning on pressure cooking the stew, then it is certainly worth using the unhulled barley.

> *Ingredients for pressure cooking:*
> ½ cup brown lentils, soaked for 2 to 3 hours
> 1 ounce unhulled barley, soaked overnight
> 1 medium tomato, quartered
> 3 cups of filtered water
> Freshly ground black pepper to taste
> Sea salt to taste

Thoroughly rinse the lentils and the barley before placing them in the cooker along with the tomatoes, black pepper, water, and sea salt. Pressure cook it for 25 minutes.

Ingredients for Sautéing:

1 small yellow onion, diced

1 small red bell pepper, chopped into bite size
    pieces

1 large carrot, thinly sliced

½ teaspoon red chili flakes

1 teaspoon fresh sweet marjoram, minced

1. Place a large skillet on high heat, add the onions
   and sauté for a minute. Turn off heat but continue
   keeping the skillet on the stovetop. Sprinkle black
   pepper, mix well, and let it sit.
2. In the meantime, chop the bell peppers and the
   carrots.
3. Turn the heat on the skillet (with the onions) back
   on to high, add the carrots, bell pepper, red chili
   flakes, and sprinkle a small quantity of water (¾
   teaspoon to 1 tablespoon) over the veggies. Mix
   well, reduce heat to medium, cover the skillet, and
   cook for 3 to 4 minutes. Carefully watch so that the
   veggies don't burn, reducing heat if necessary. Turn
   off heat and mix the sweet marjoram into the veggies
   and set aside.
4. Add the cooked lentils and barley into the sautéed
   veggies and serve.

*Note: You can substitute spelt berries for barley. I suggest that
you soak the spelt over night as well.*

*Sautéing onions for just a minute and letting them sit
for 5 minutes or so seems to enhance the overall flavor.*

Savory Lentil Crepes

PREPARATION TIME: 20 MINUTES

This south Indian dish, traditional known as "adai" in Tamil, is an absolute favorite of ours. So much so that my husband, Russill, can prepare it without much assistance from me. As a matter of fact, he does a better job than me, as his crepes are perfectly shaped and crispy.

Mung beans are highly regarded in Ayurveda, the holistic healing system of India. They are gently healing and detoxing, and favored by all body types ("doshas").

I have personally benefited tremendous by including mung beans into my diet, especially during my periods, and have had wonderful results—a gentler flow and better digestion. As you may already know, digestion during the menstrual cycle can become very fragile. In my experience, nourishing the body with simple, wholefoods is one of the keys to a healthier period.

Traditionally in Tamil Nadu, adias (crepe) are mostly white rice, with a small amount of lentils. The ratio is generally 3:1, the quantity of rice being 3 parts to 1 part lentils.

I do the reverse, and hence my adais are predominately mung bean, and the batter is a beautiful green!

The combination of brown rice with mung beans makes this dish a complete protein-rich food. Enjoy!

Ingredients for blending:
1 cup green mung beans
1 ounce yellow or green spilt peas
1 ounce brown rice
½ teaspoon asafetida powder
6 whole black peppercorns (reduce quantity
    for less heat)
2 dried red chilies, stems removed (reduce
    quantity for a milder version)
Sea salt to taste
Ingredients to add once the batter is made:
1 teaspoon cumin seeds, ground into a fine
    powder
¼ teaspoon fenugreek seeds, ground into
    a fine powder
2 cups red onions, finely diced
A handful of cilantro leaves, minced

Oil for making the crepe:
Extra virgin olive oil or avocado oil or
    virgin coconut oil

1. Place the mung beans, split peas, and the brown rice in a non-reactive dish, add 4 to 5 cups of filtered water, cover the dish, and let it soak overnight. When ready to prepare the adais, discard the soaking water by pouring the beans and the brown rice into a colander, rinse well, and shake off the excess water.
2. Place all the batter ingredients in a blender and blend until somewhat coarse. Make sure it is not finely ground. To ensure this, add small quantities of filtered water while blending.
3. Add the chopped red onions, powdered cumin and fenugreek seeds, and the cilantro to the batter and mix well.
4. Place a cast iron griddle pan on high heat for 1 to 2 minutes. Once the pan is hot, lightly coat the surface of the pan with oil, pour in a ladle of the batter, and spread it around. Cook each side for 2 to 3 minutes. Serve hot.

Khichdi

PREPARATION TIME: 15 MINUTES
COOKING TIME: 35 MINUTES

"Khichdi," or "khichuri," is a popular northern Indian dish, which is a hearty and wholesome one-pot meal. Made from a combination of rice and lentils, it is a wholesome comfort food.

As mentioned above, rice is traditionally used to make this dish, and the ratio of rice to lentils is 2:1; that is, 1 cup of rice and ½ cup of lentils. In my version of the khichdi, I substitute millet for rice and use a variety of beans. I also add sambar powder, which is a quintessential south Indian spice mixture that you can easily obtain from any Indian grocery store.

Ingredients:
2 ounces mung beans
2 ounces adzuki beans
1 ounce brown lentils
1 ounce green split peas
2 ounces unhulled millet
3½ cups filtered water
1 teaspoon cumin seeds
½ teaspoon turmeric powder
½ teaspoon asafetida powder
¾ teaspoon sambar powder
Sea salt to taste
1 teaspoon extra virgin olive oil

Ingredients for seasoning:
1 teaspoon mustard seeds
1 teaspoon ginger, peeled and minced
1 teaspoon virgin coconut or avocado oil
Freshly ground black pepper (optional)

1. Place the beans and the millet in a non-reactive dish, add 5 to 7 cups of filtered water, cover the dish, and let it soak overnight or for a minimum of 7 hours. When ready to cook, discard the soaking water by pouring the beans and the millet into a colander, rinse well, shake off the excess water, and set aside.

2. Place a medium-sized stainless steel soup pot on medium-high heat for about 30 to 45 seconds. When the pot is hot, add the cumin seeds and begin to roast them for about 30 seconds, be careful not to let them burn. As the aroma wafts from the seeds, turn off heat and add 1 teaspoon of olive oil and, with a swirling motion, coat the pan with the oil. Add the spices, millet, lentils, mung beans, and sea salt to taste. Mix the grains and the beans with the spices. Increase the heat, from medium to high, add water, and bring it to a rolling boil. Reduce heat to simmer, cover the pot, and let it cook for 45 minutes. The cooked dish will have a thick stew-like consistency, neither too dry nor too watery.

3. On a separate cast iron skillet, pop the mustard seeds, reduce heat, add the ginger, coconut or avocado oil, and sauté on low heat for about 1 minute. Add freshly ground black pepper (optional), remove from heat, and add it to the cooked beans and millet, mixing well. Serve hot.

Note: The millet has a tendency to stick to the bottom of the pot. Make sure to cook it over a very low heat and keep an eye mid-way through, so as not to burn the dish.

Postscript

It is my hope that this book makes your library of favorites, and is referred to often.

It does indeed take a village to create a book! Apart from the credits provided to the amazing people who have assisted me in making this book possible, I would like to acknowledge two other caring and loving friends who agreed to proofread this work in its infancy. They are Br. Gregory Perron and Timothy Hellner. Thank you, you kind and gracious gentlemen, for your time, love, and support. And thank you my darling Russill, for your gentle yet valuable critique, and most importantly, for being my devoted cheerleader throughout this process. I love you!

My expertise lies in helping my clients thrive and feel their best, not just through food alone, but by helping them perceive the extraordinary power of the human brain and the mind. Having a healthy body image together with effective weight management and addressing stress-related issues are my specialty. However, as an integrative nutrition health coach, I address every aspect of my client's life, including relationships, career, or life purpose if the person is retired. Towards this end I create a safe space in which both women and men can get in touch with their innate wisdom to create their best life yet in ways that feel authentic for them. Each session is therefore tailored to an individual's specific goals and needs. For a more extensive understanding of what I offer through my coaching programs, please visit my website **ashapaul.com**.

Do look out for my next book in the Blissful Mouthful series.

Wishing you Happy Cooking and Healthy Eating!

ENDNOTES

1 http://solutions.naifa.org/majority-of-women-now-responsible-for-household-finances, by Ayo Mseka on Jan 24, 2018 9:00:00 AM

2 https://www.cnbc.com/2017/09/27/how-much-americans-waste-on-dining-out.html Emmie Martin | @emmiemartin 9:39 AM ET Wed, 27 Sept 2017

3 http://adelledavis.org/quotations/.

4 https://www.hsph.harvard.edu/nutritionsource/2007/04/26/ask-the-expert-controlling-your-weight/

5 https://www.pbs.org/newshour/health/silly-rabbit-junk-food-ads-contribute-to-childhood-obesity-study-says https://www.preventioninstitute.org/focus-areas/were-not-buying-it-get-involved/were-not-buying-it-the-facts-on-junk-food-marketing-and-kids

6 is a core concept created by Joshua Rosenthal the founder of IIN which is proven true scientifically.

7 https://www.researchgate.net/publication/325751215_History_of_modern_nutrition_science-implications_for_current_research_dietary_guidelines_and_food_policy

8 https://www.vox.com/2016/1/14/10760622/nutrition-science-complicated

INDEX

RECIPE INDEX

Author's Bio

Asha Paul is a Health and Spiritual Coach.

As a graduate of the Institute for Integrative Nutrition, she has studied over 100 dietary theories, practical lifestyle and stress-management techniques, along with ingenious coaching methods from some of the world's top health and wellness experts today.

She helps her clients thrive and feel their best by integrating leading-edge discoveries such as epigenesis, neuroplasticity, and the new psychology in her coaching plans.

She is also a dedicated meditation practitioner. Her unique coaching approach lies in her faith for the human potential that goes beyond mere optimism.

As a conscious entrepreneur, she has launched, sustained, and grown a successful business from the ground up, providing excellent service to clients and students alike.

Asha lives in Austin, TX, with her husband Russill Paul, known for his books, music records, and worldwide recognition as an expert teacher of transformative spirituality. Shortly after their marriage in 1989, they immigrated from South India to North America.

Please visit **ashapaul.com** for an extended bio and to learn more about her offerings.

Postscript

You may be pleased to know that ten percent of the profit from the sale of this book will be donated to a food bank.

It is my hope that this book makes your library of favorites and is referred to often.

It does indeed take a village to create a book! Apart from the credits provided to the amazing people who have assisted me in making this book possible, I would also like to acknowledge two more caring friends who agreed to proofread this work in its infancy. They are Br. Gregory Perron and Timothy Hellner. Thank you, you kind and gracious gentlemen, for your time, love, and support.

And thank you, my darling Russill, for your gentle yet valuable critique, and most importantly, for being my devoted cheerleader throughout this process. I love you!

Please do lookout for my next book in the *Blissful Mouthful* series.

Wishing you Happy Cooking and Healthy Eating!

Made in the USA
Las Vegas, NV
06 November 2021